A Potpourri of Pictures 2
A color Therapy Coloring Book
By
Kim Jordan Blair

I would like to thank my friend Patrick Tilley for coloring the picture on the cover of this book.

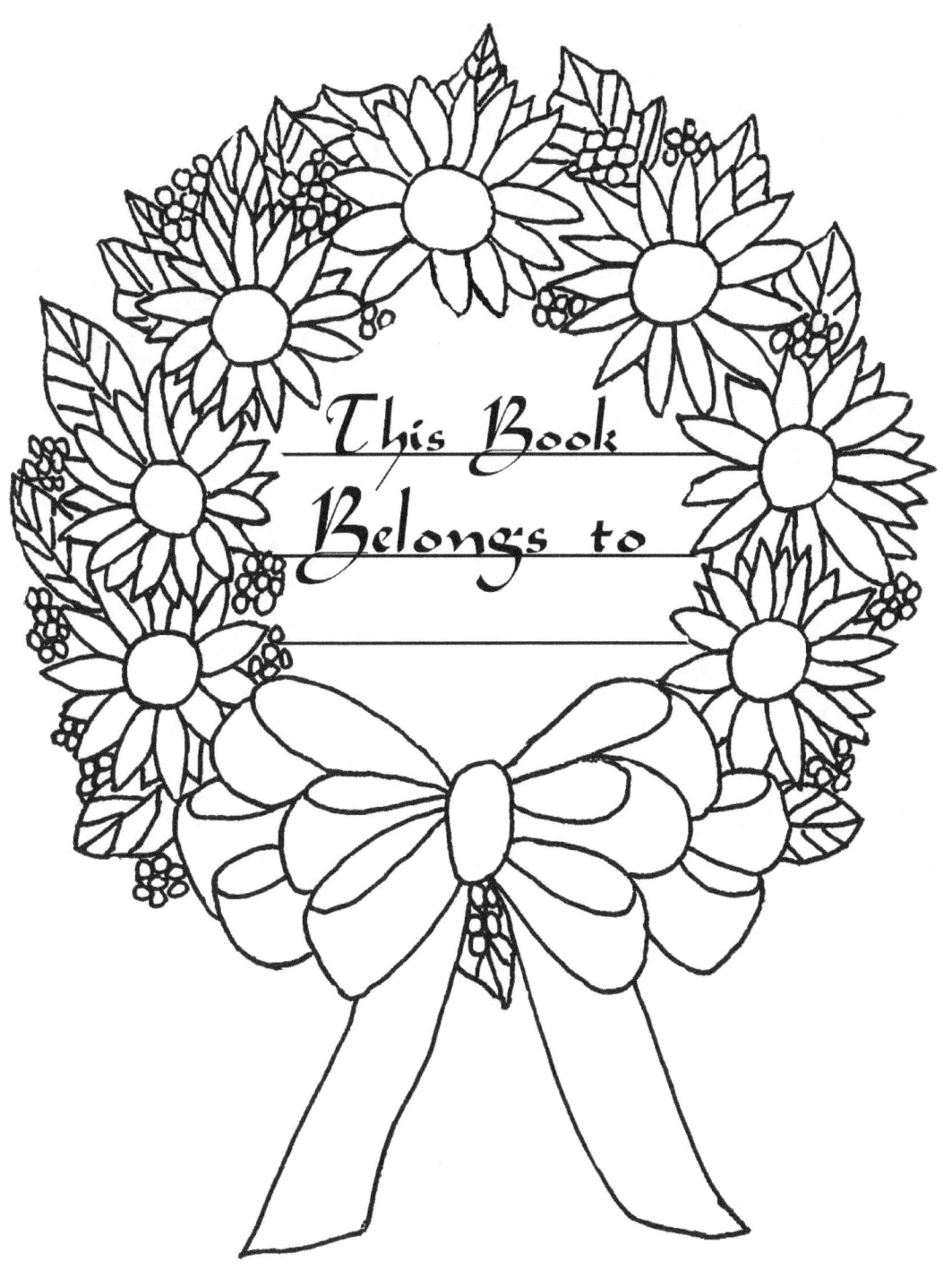

This Book

Belongs to

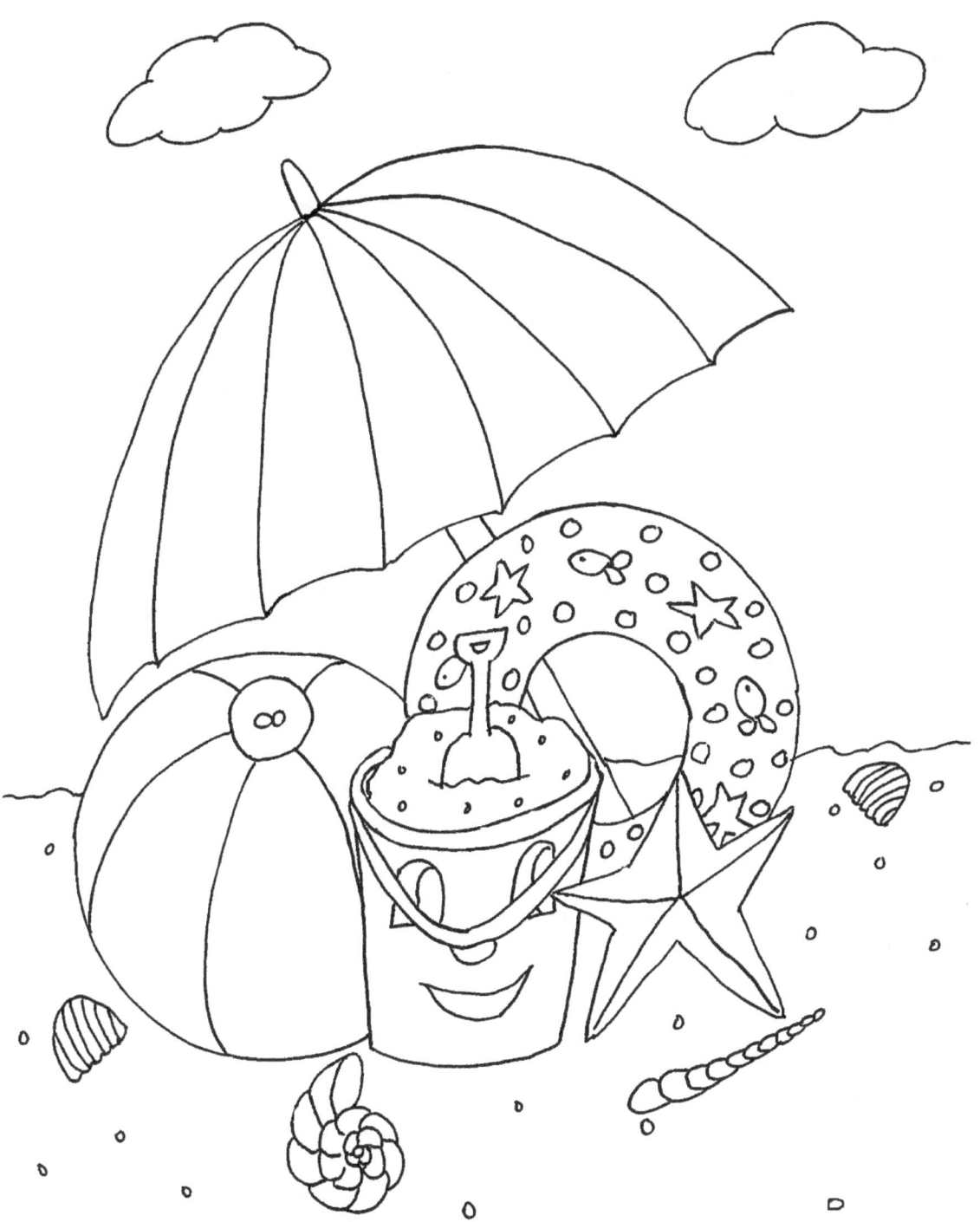

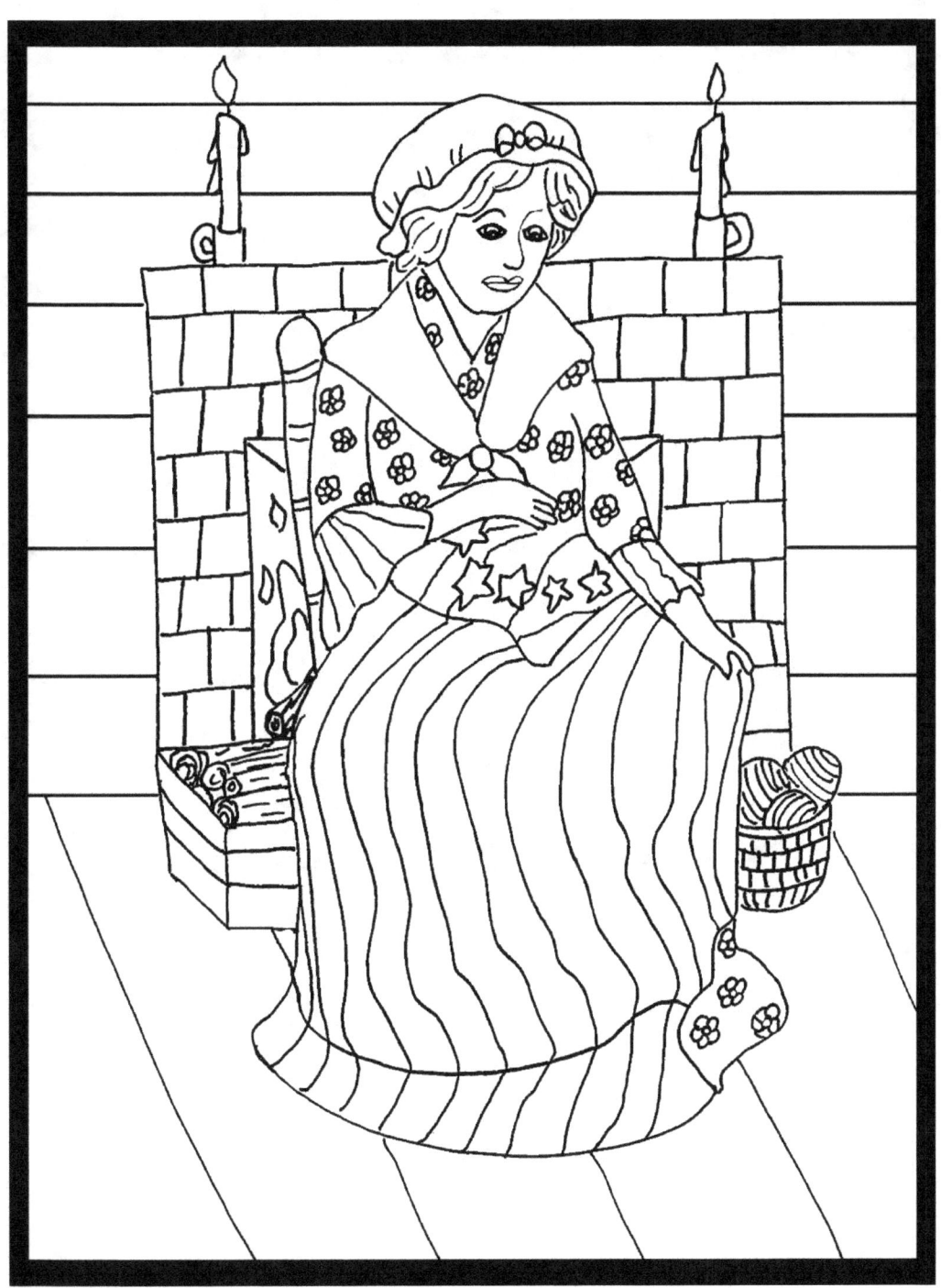

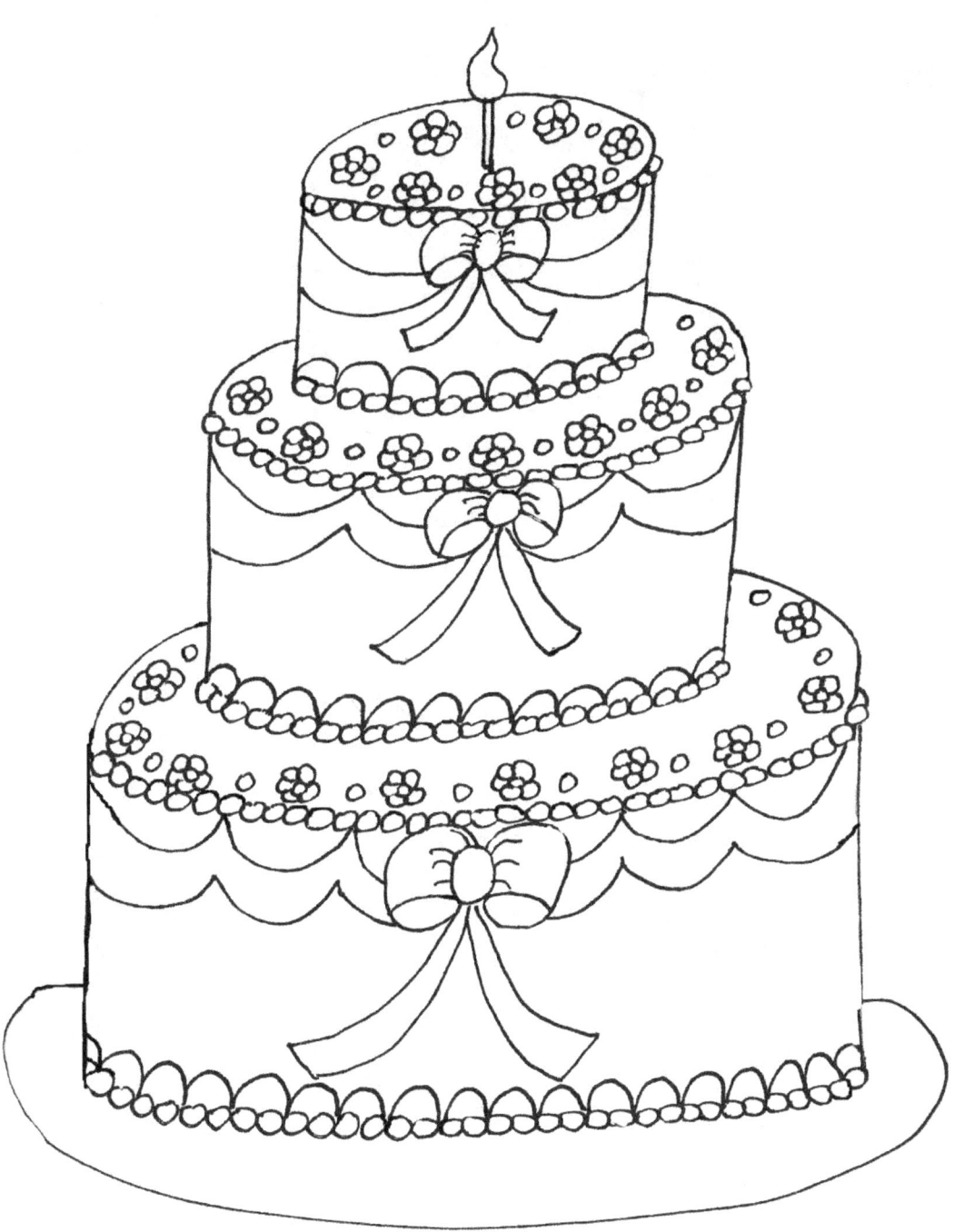

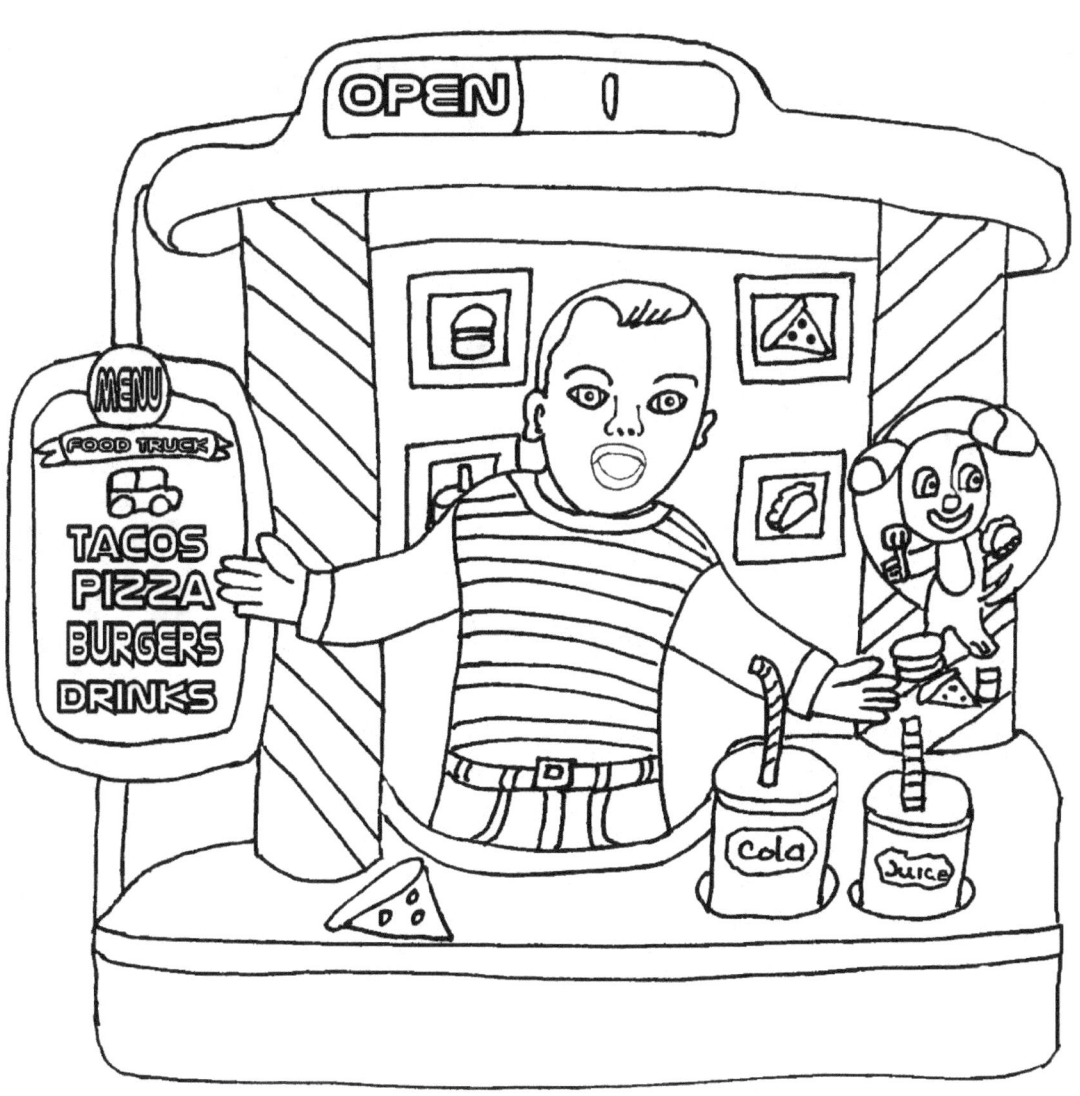

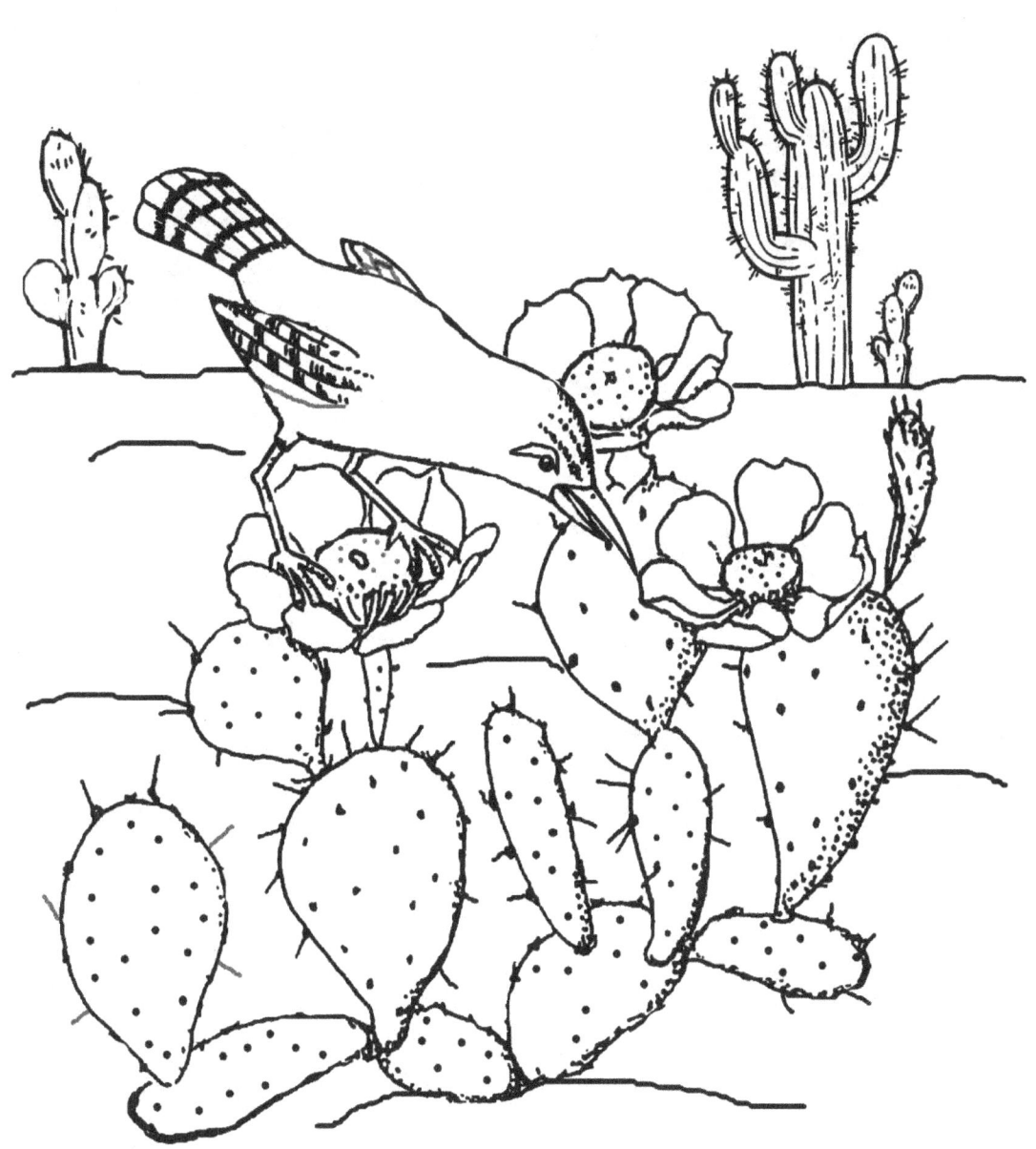

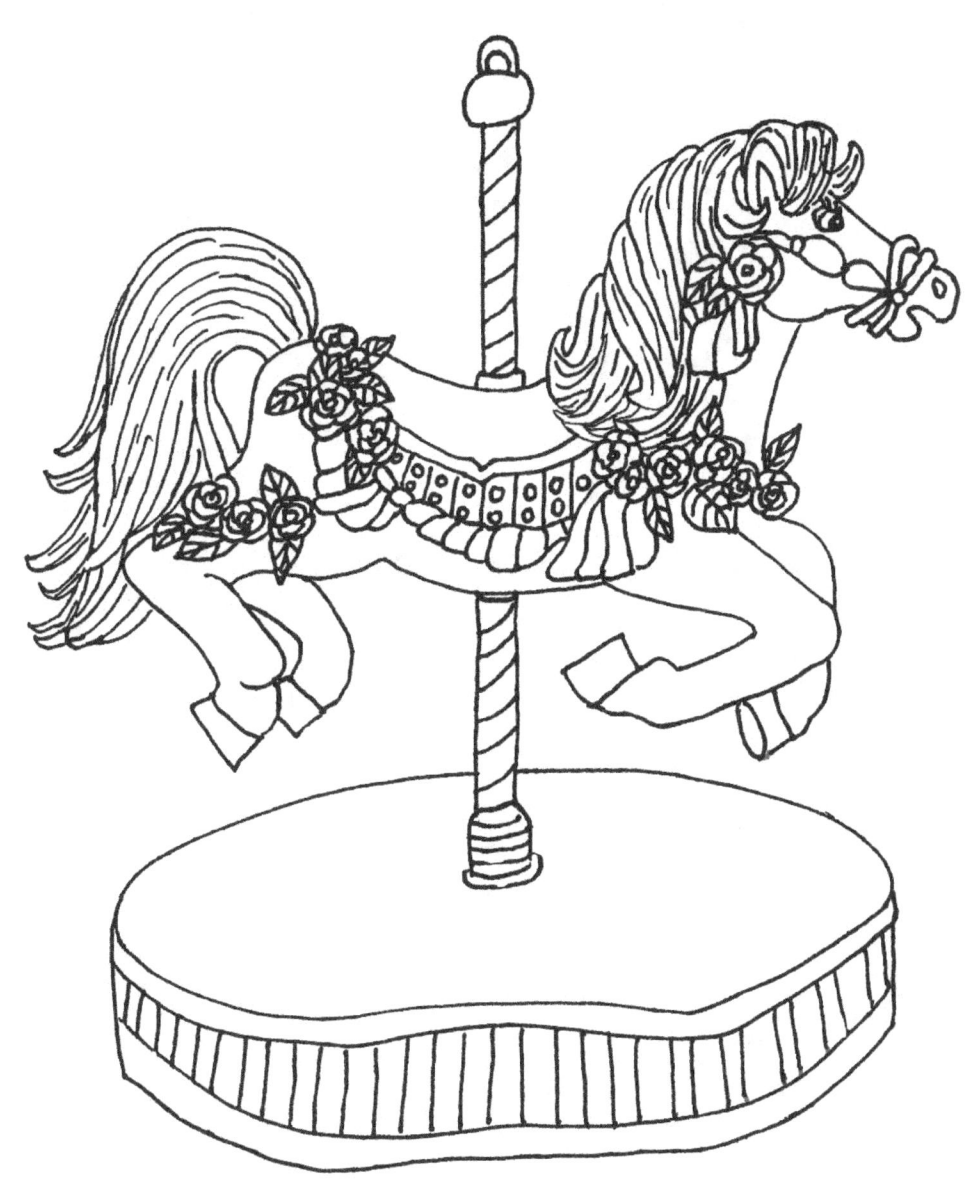

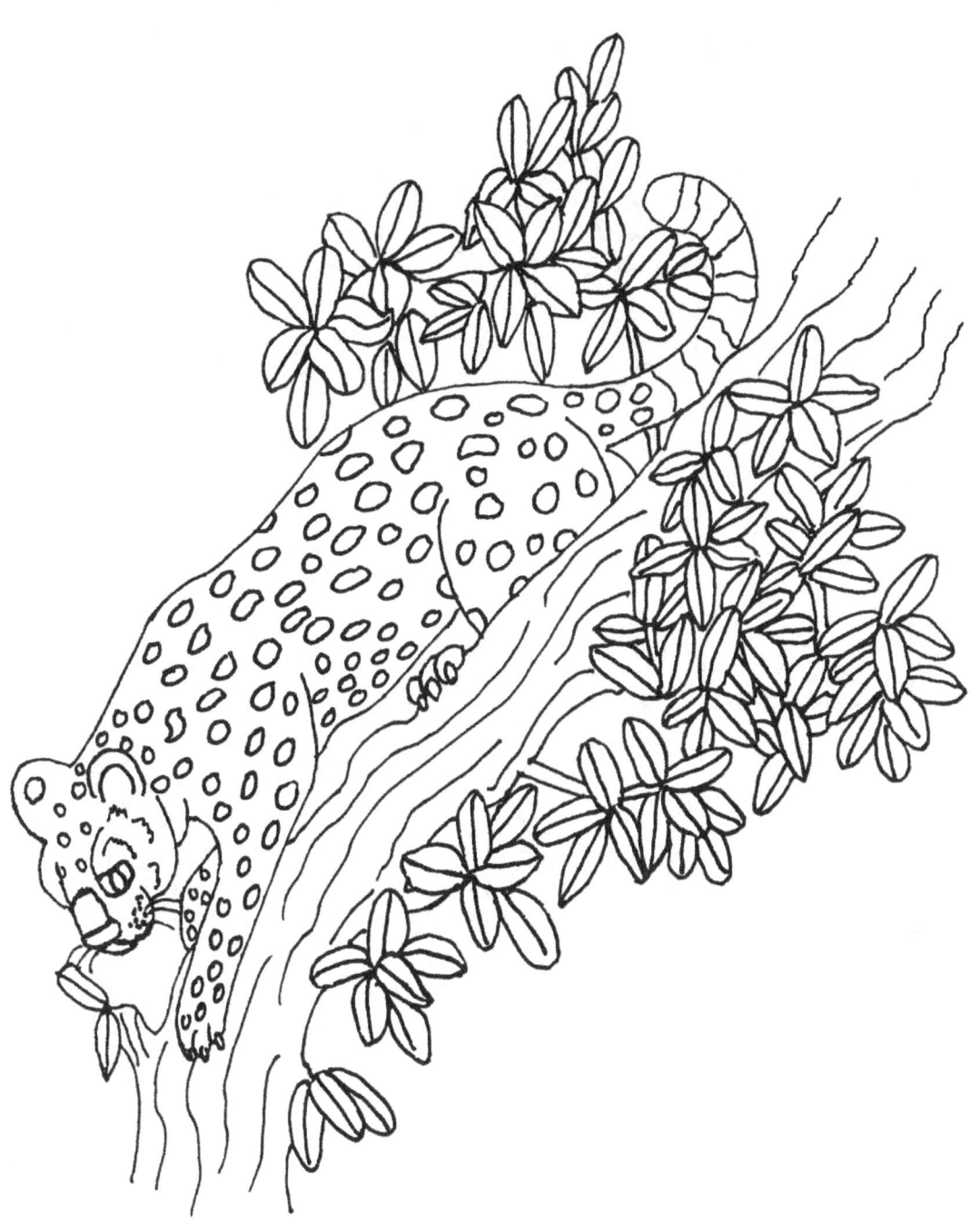

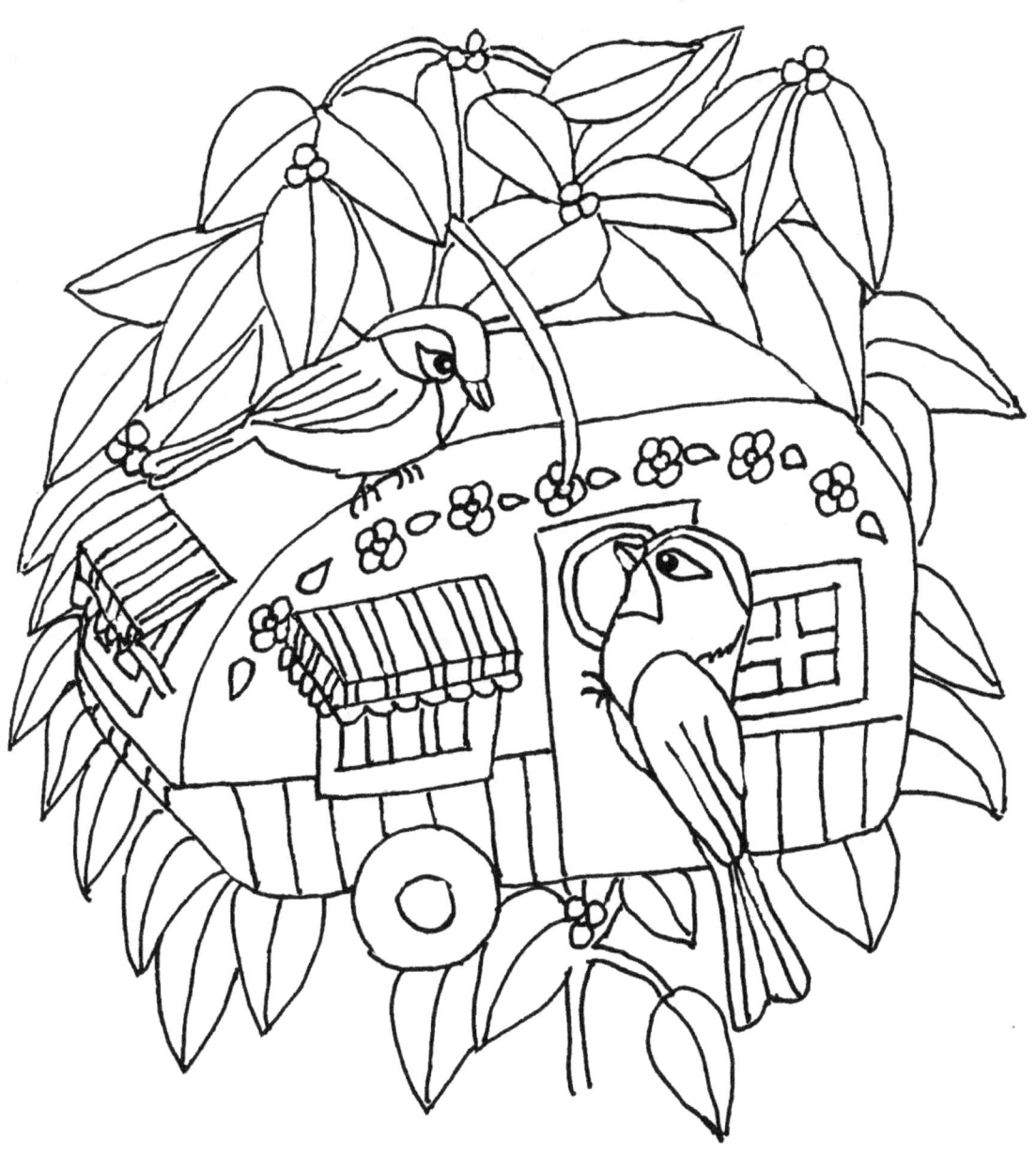

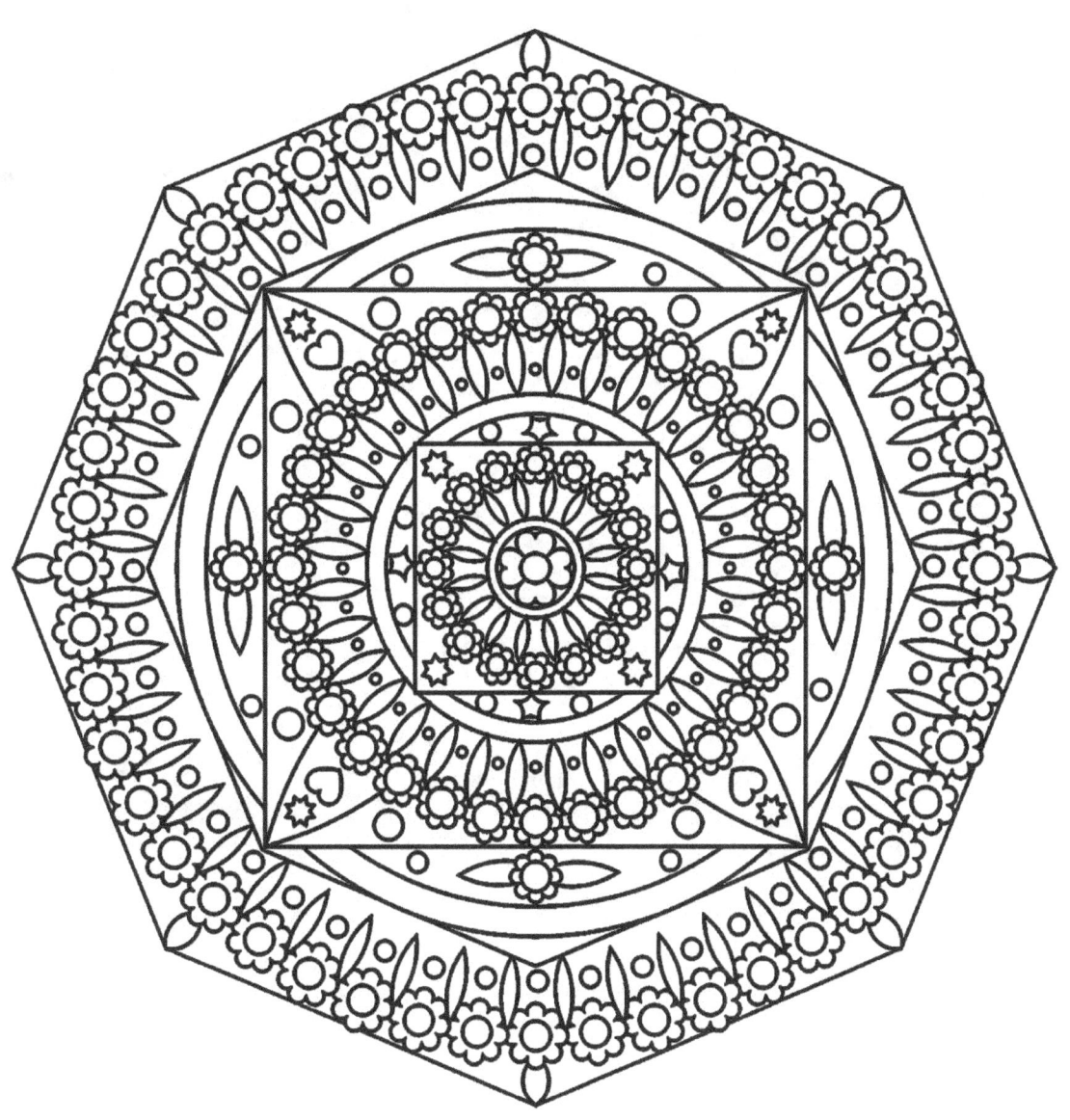

For we have all sinned and fallen

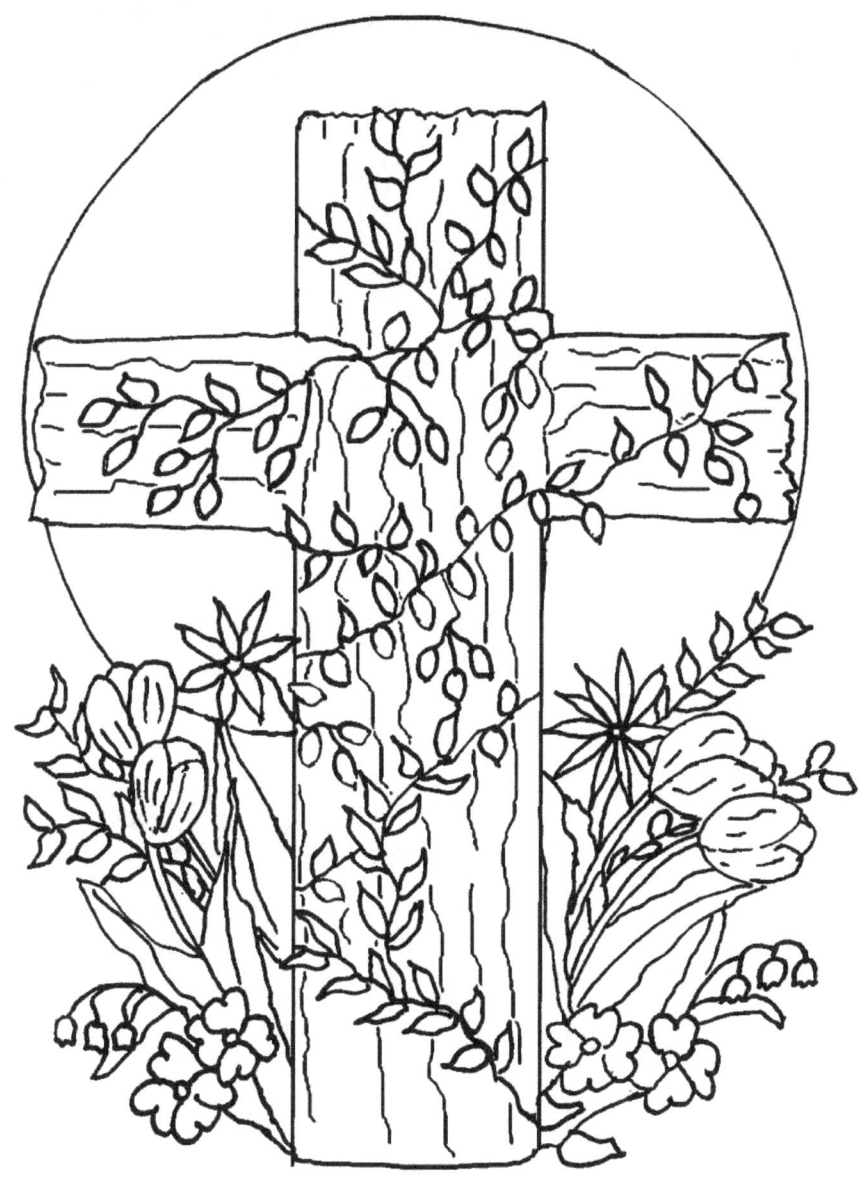

Short of the glory of God
Romans 3:23

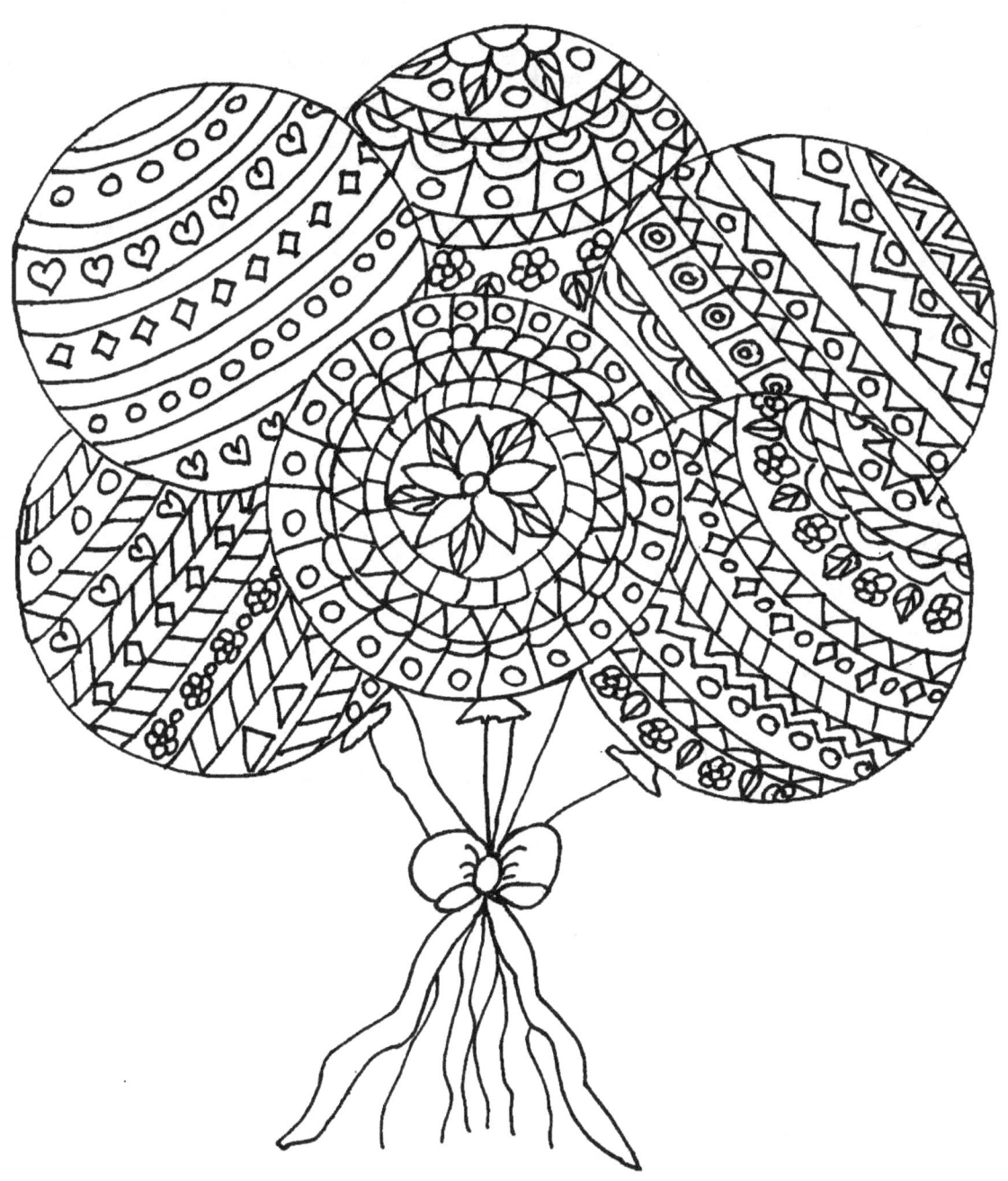

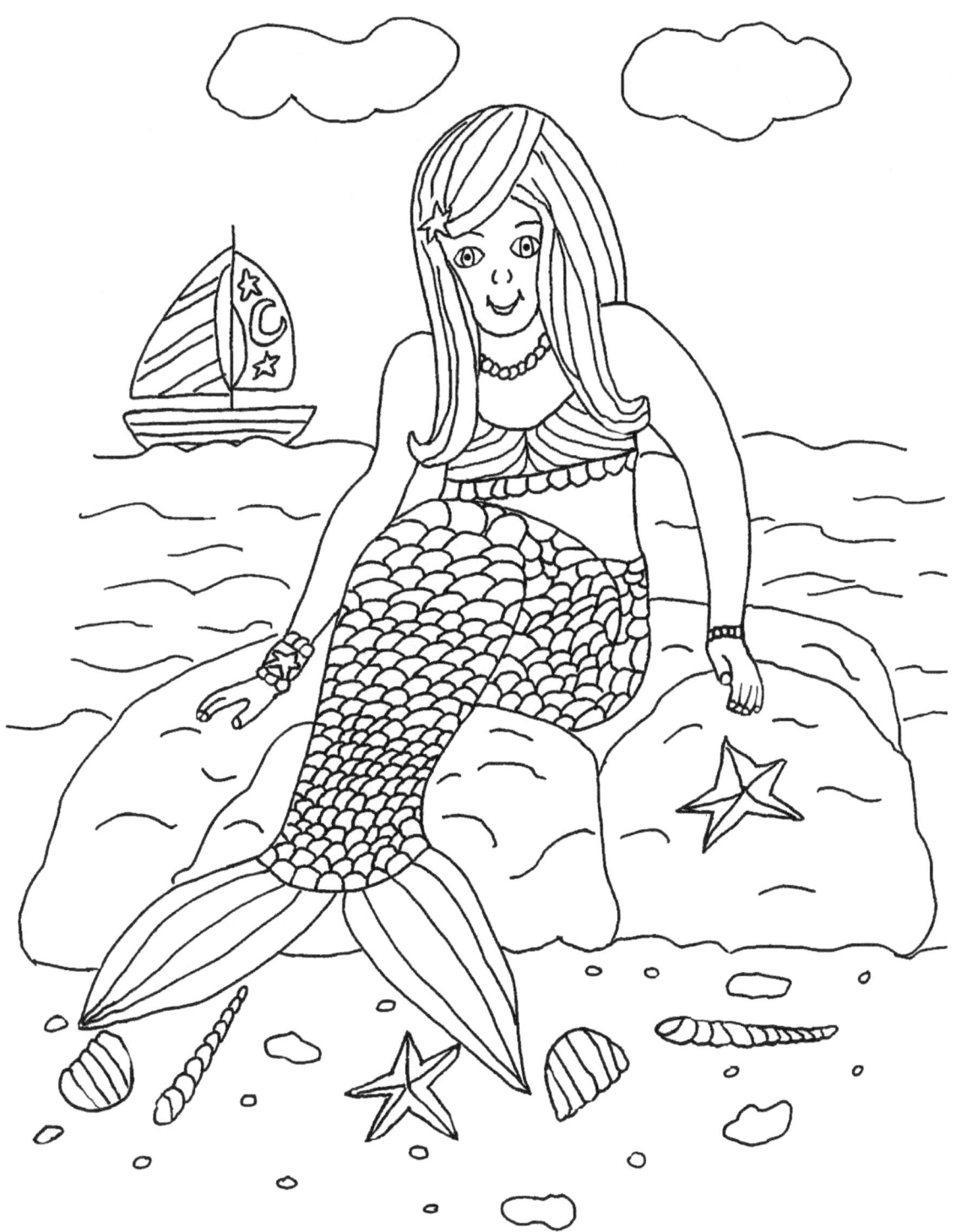

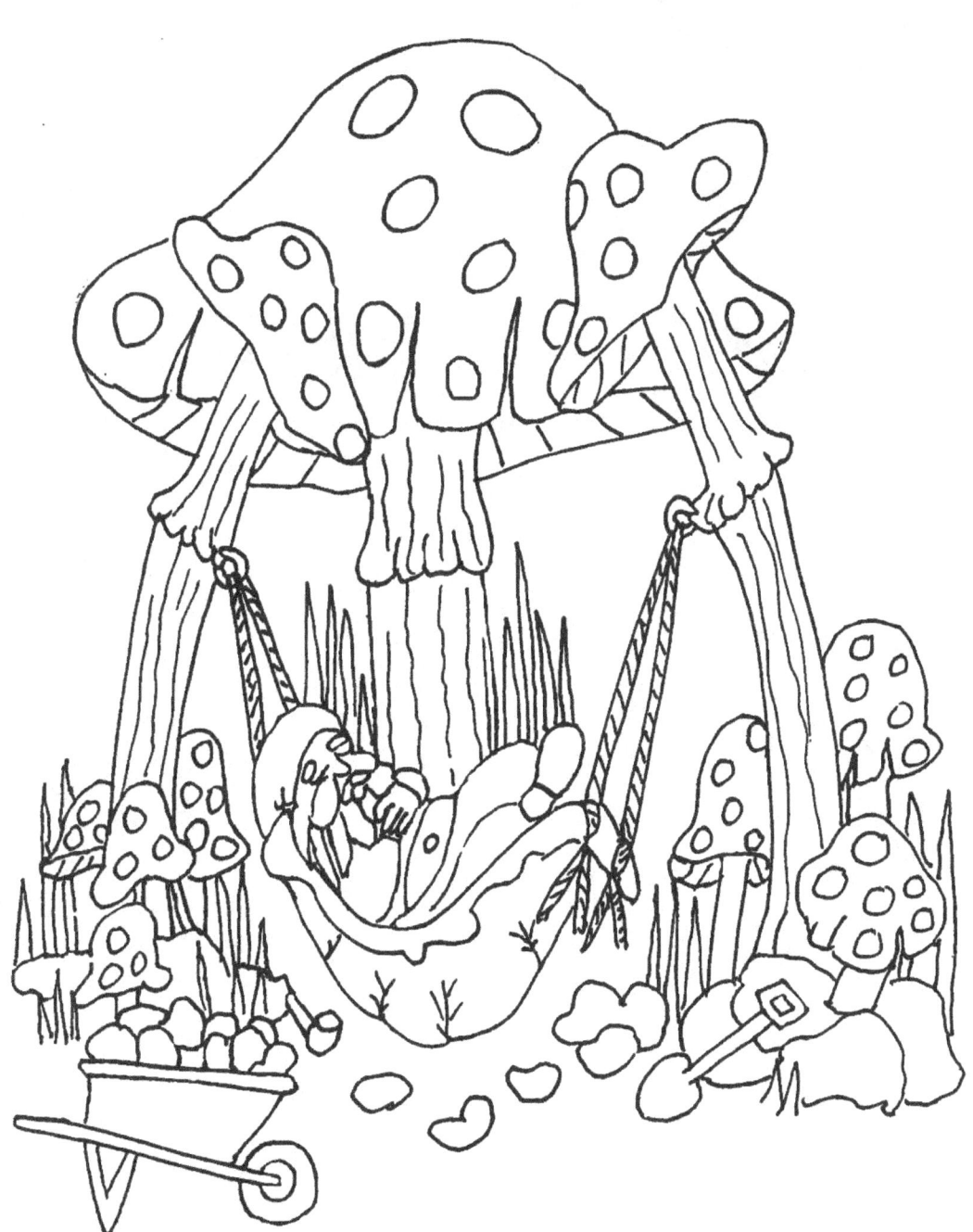

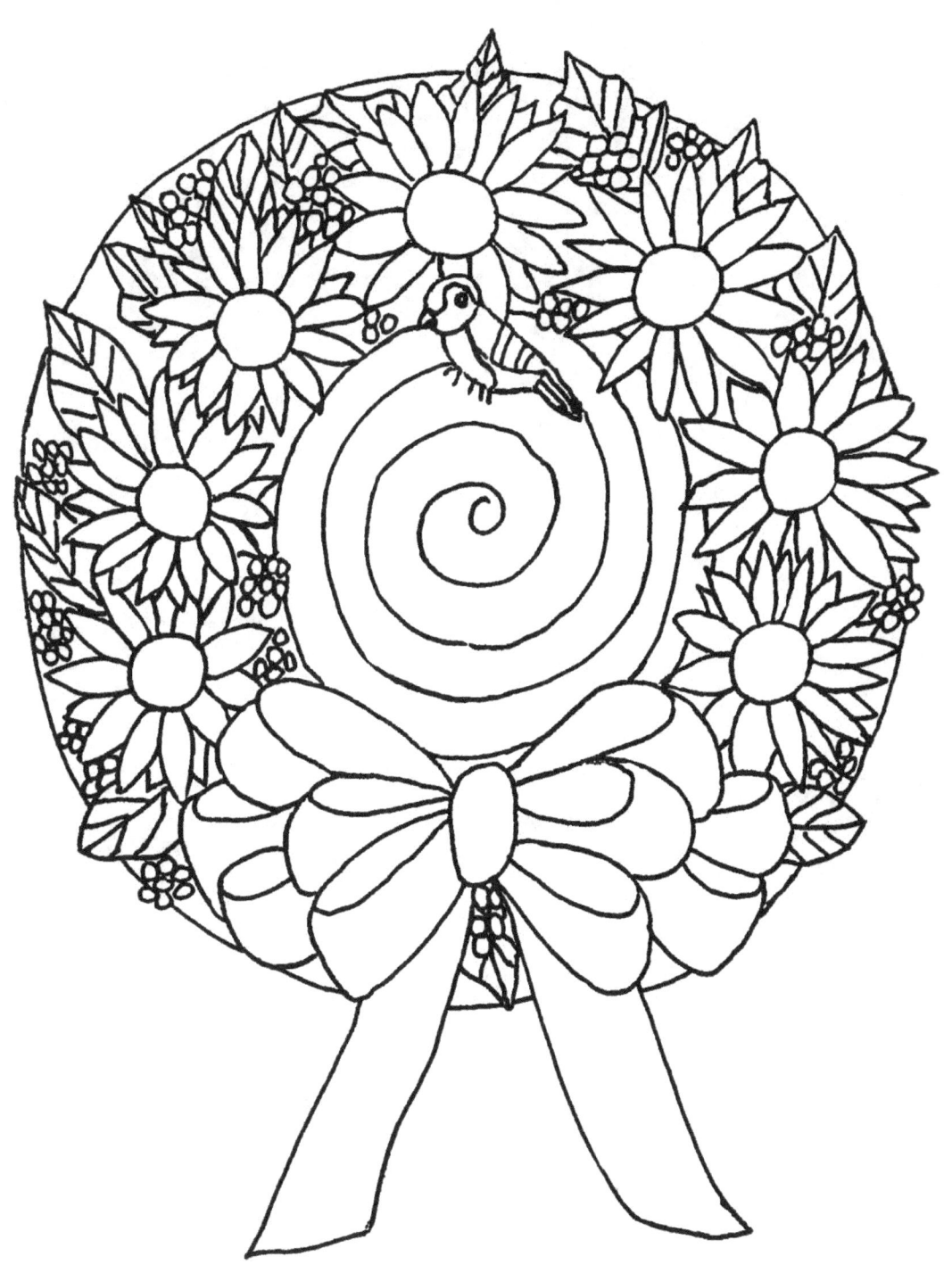

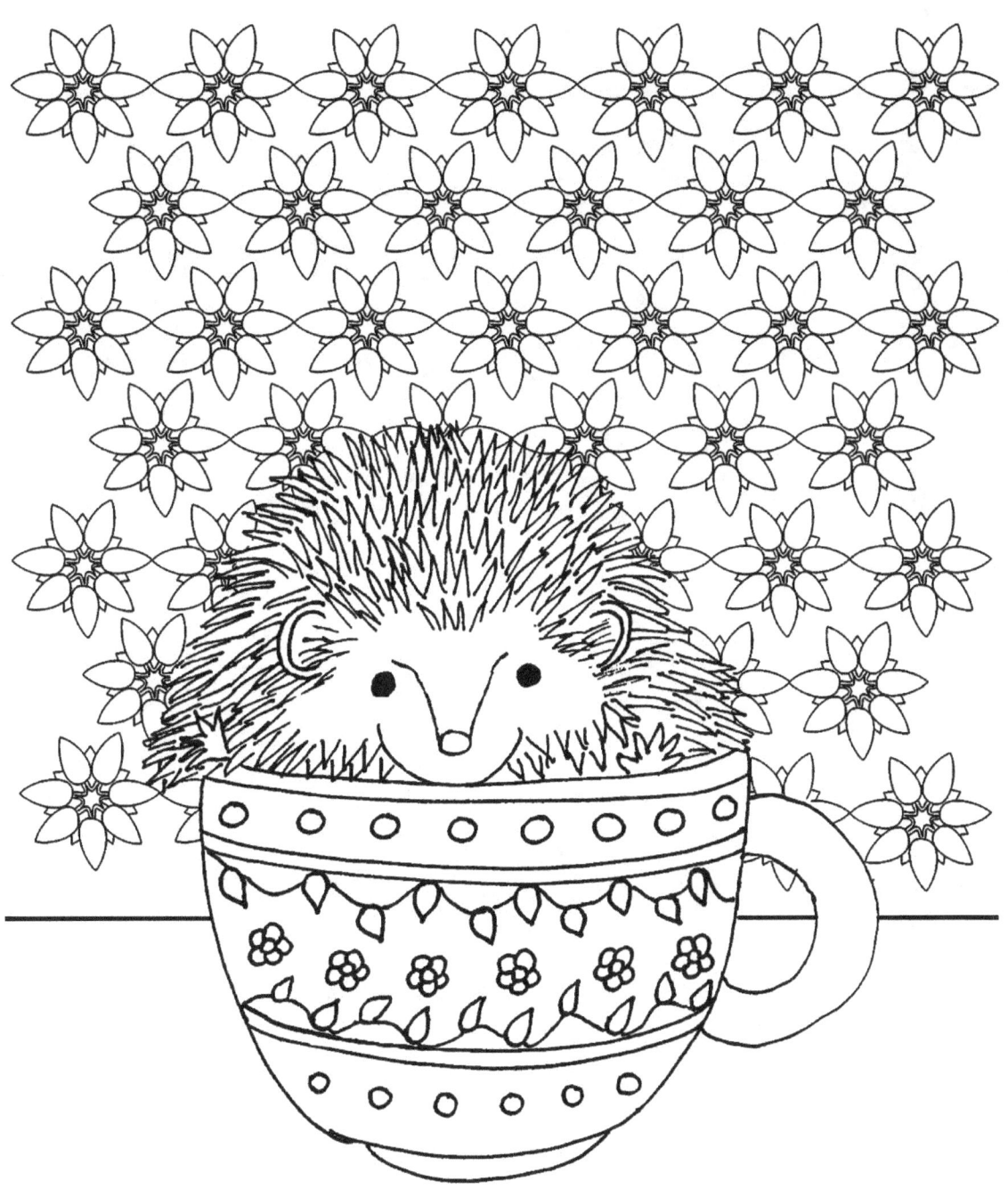

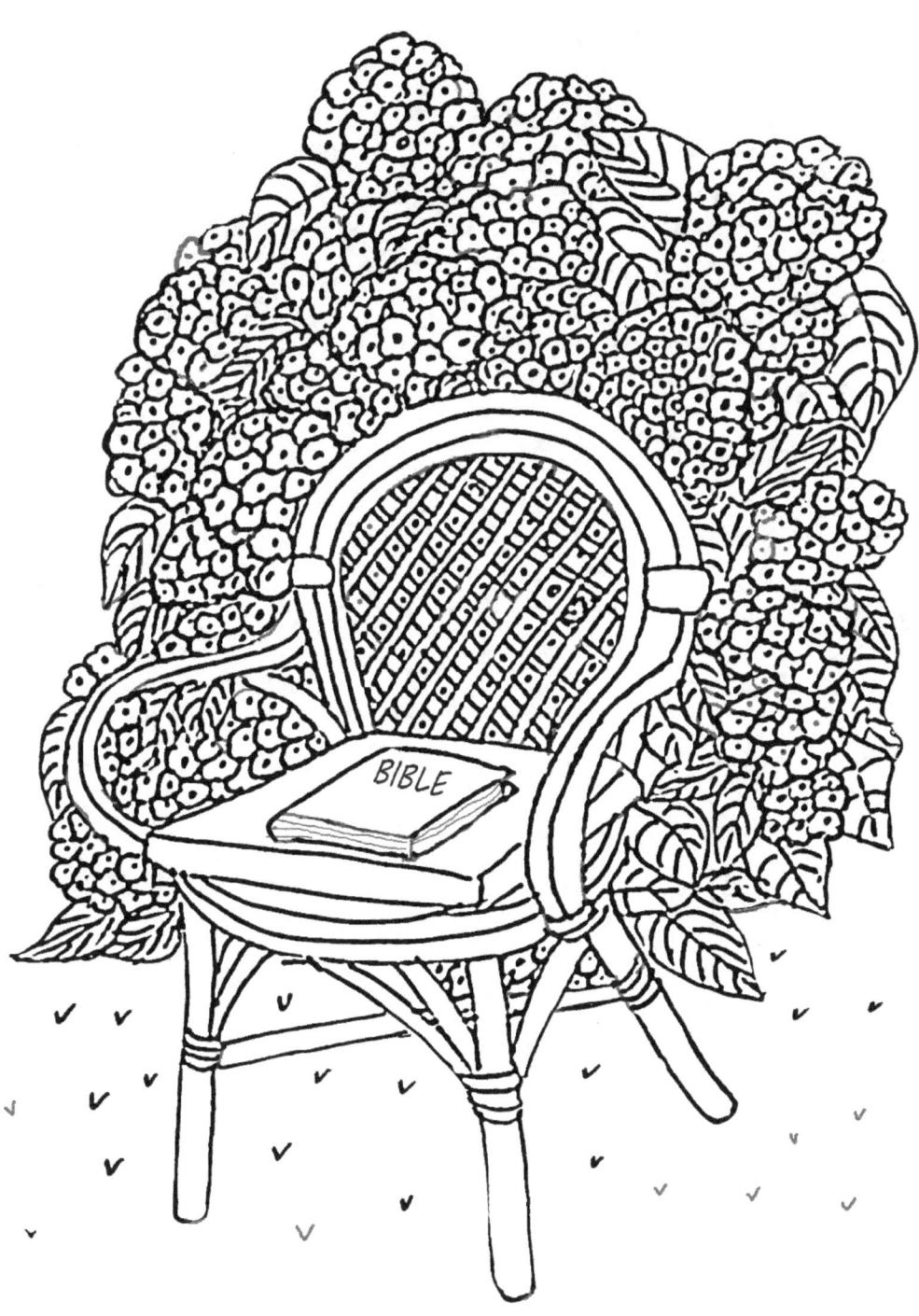

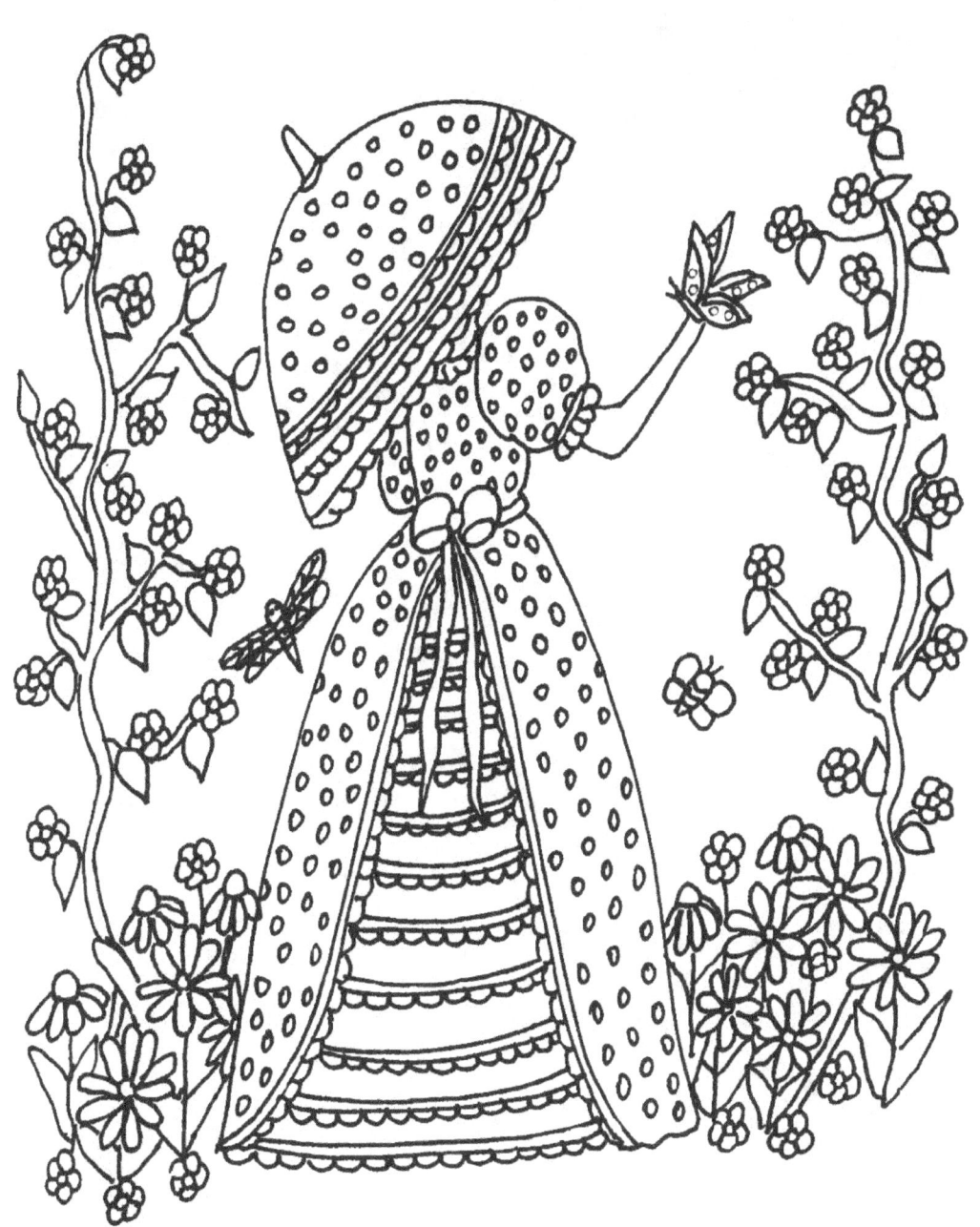

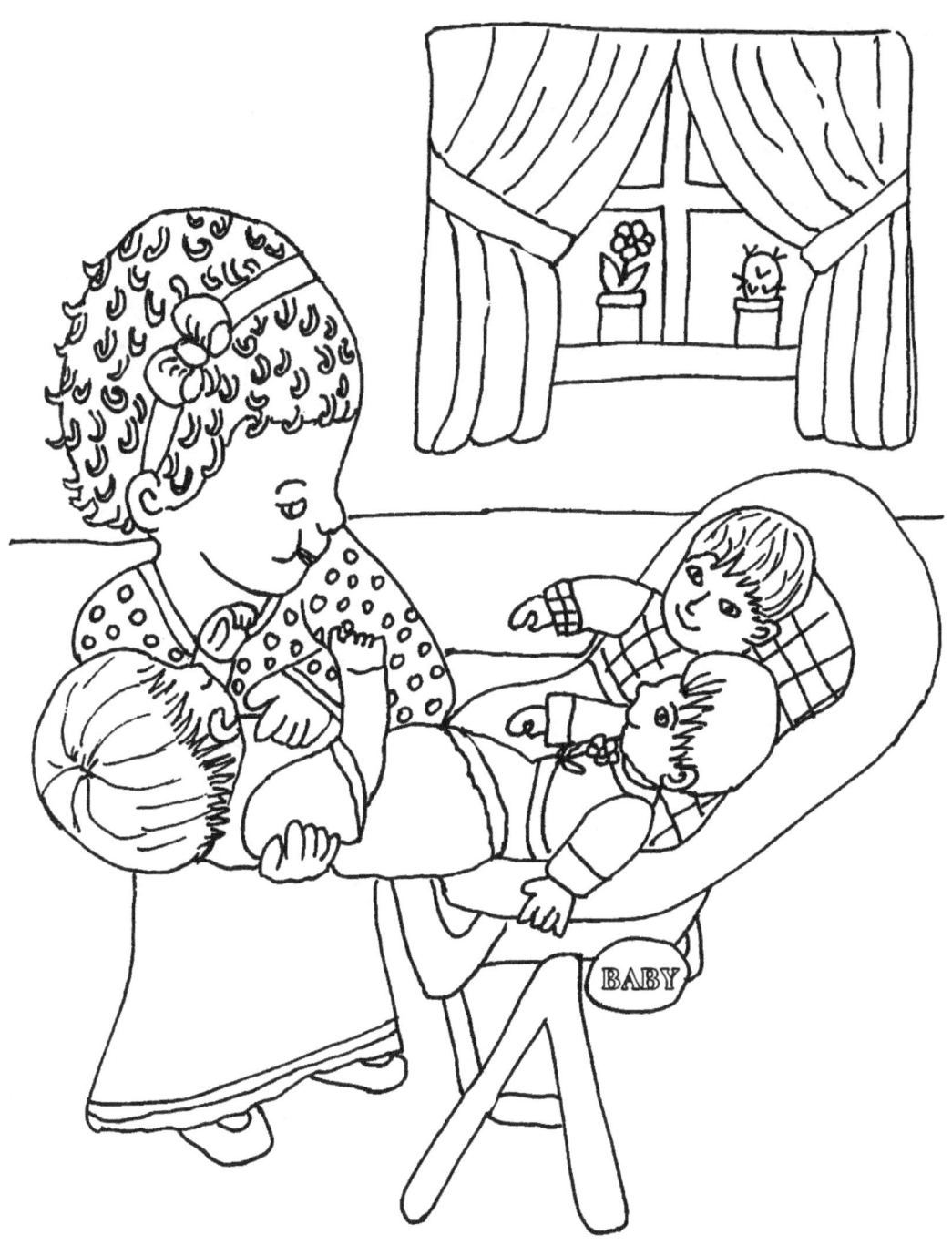

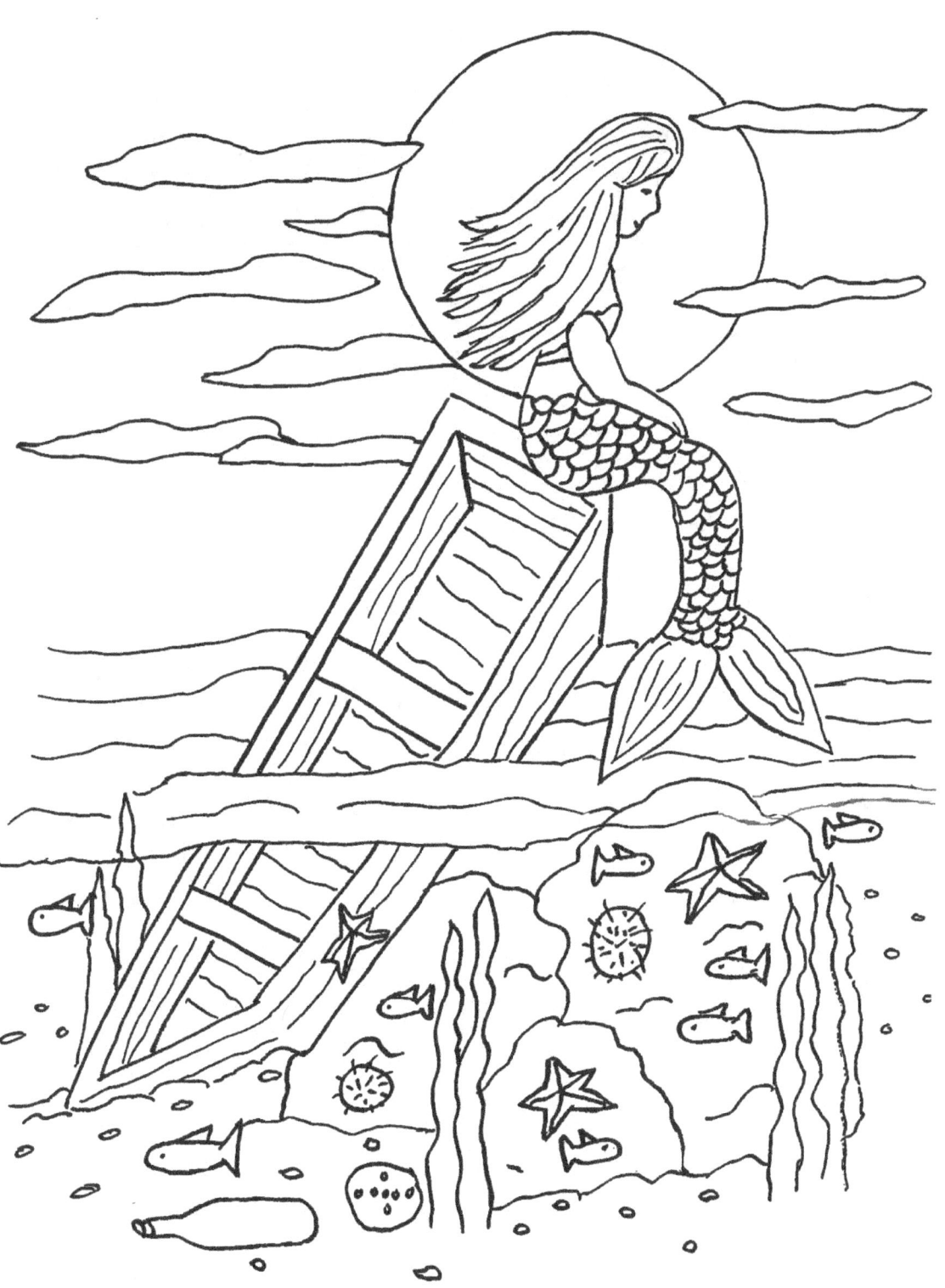

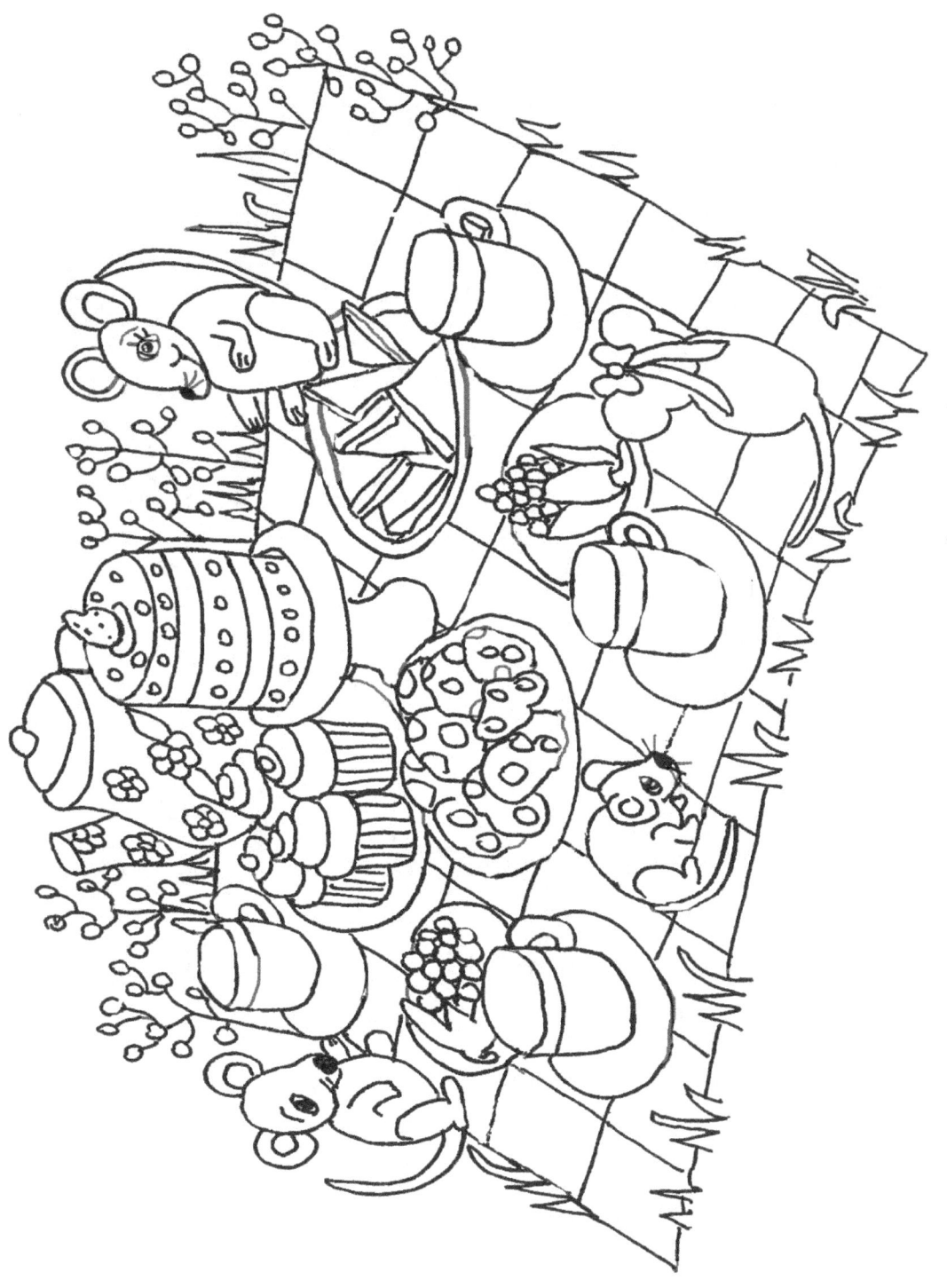

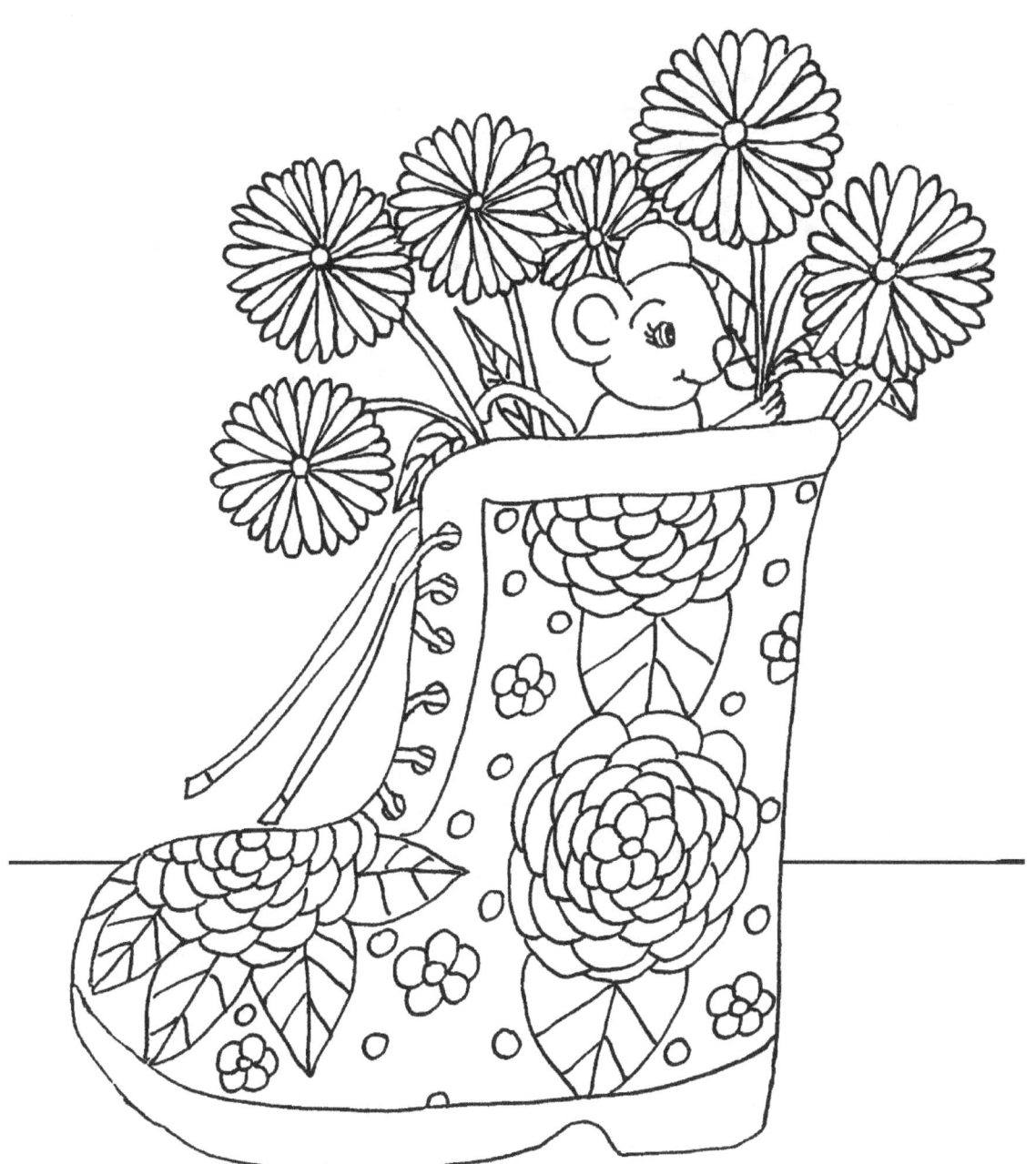

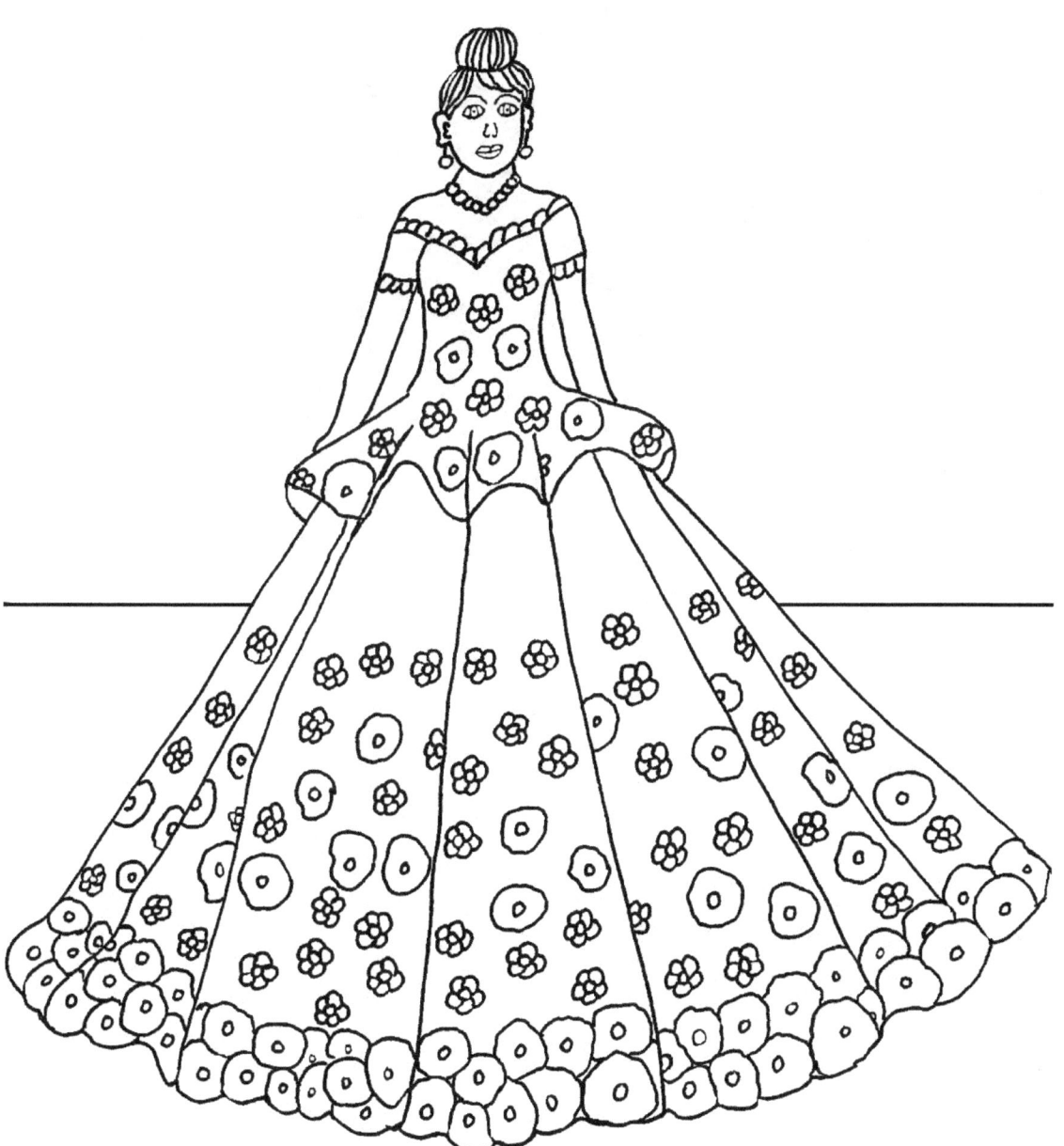

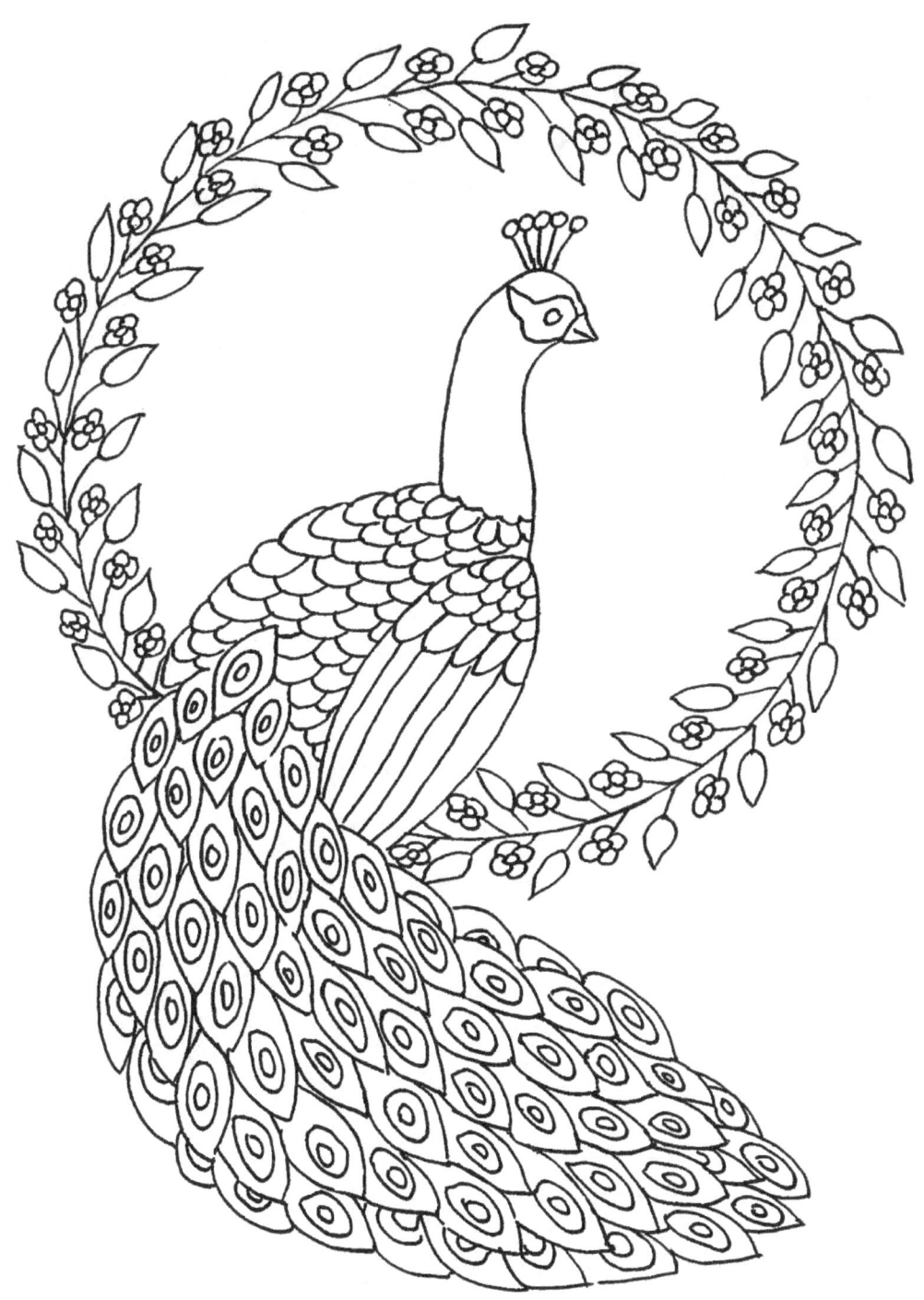

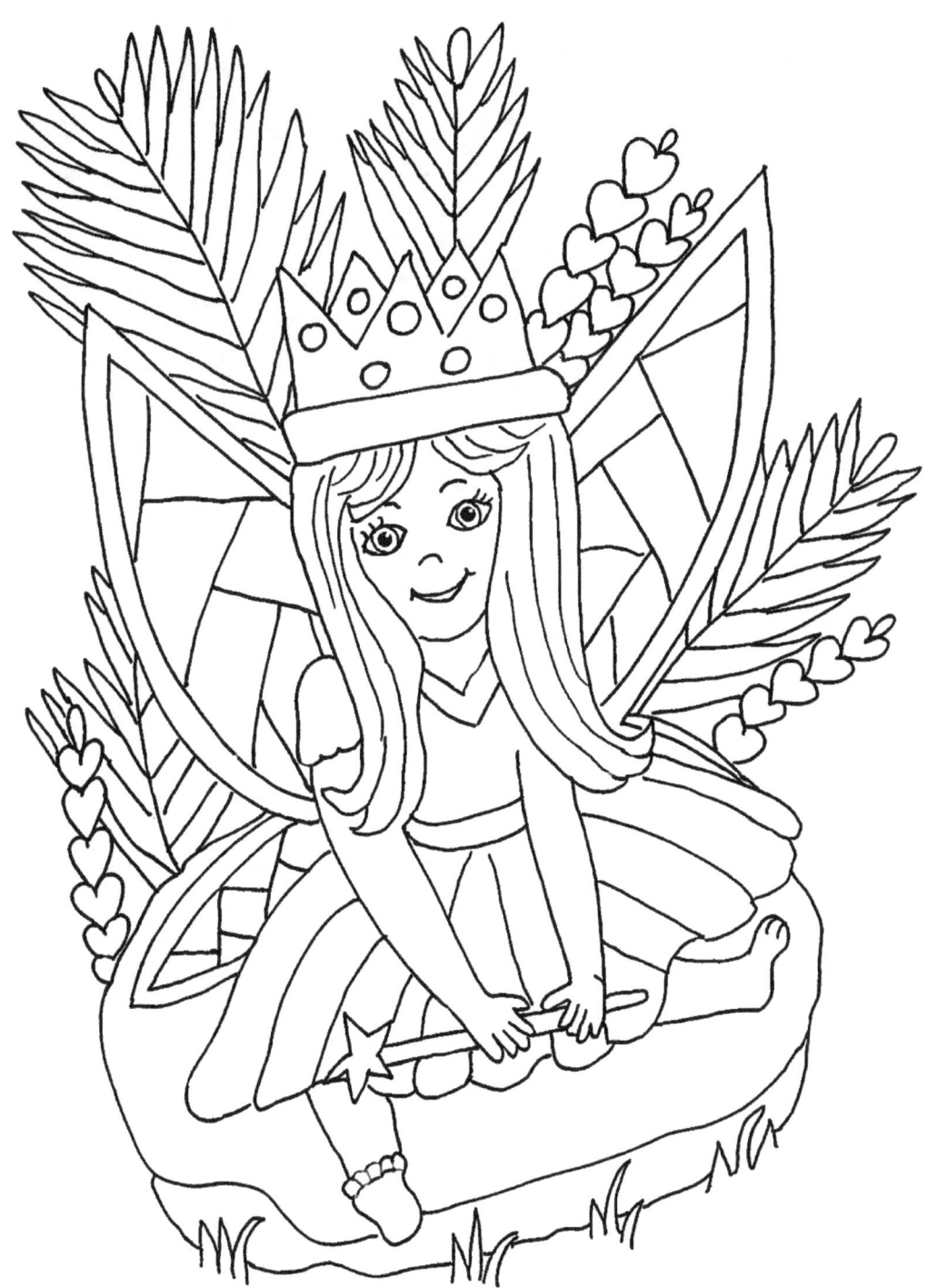

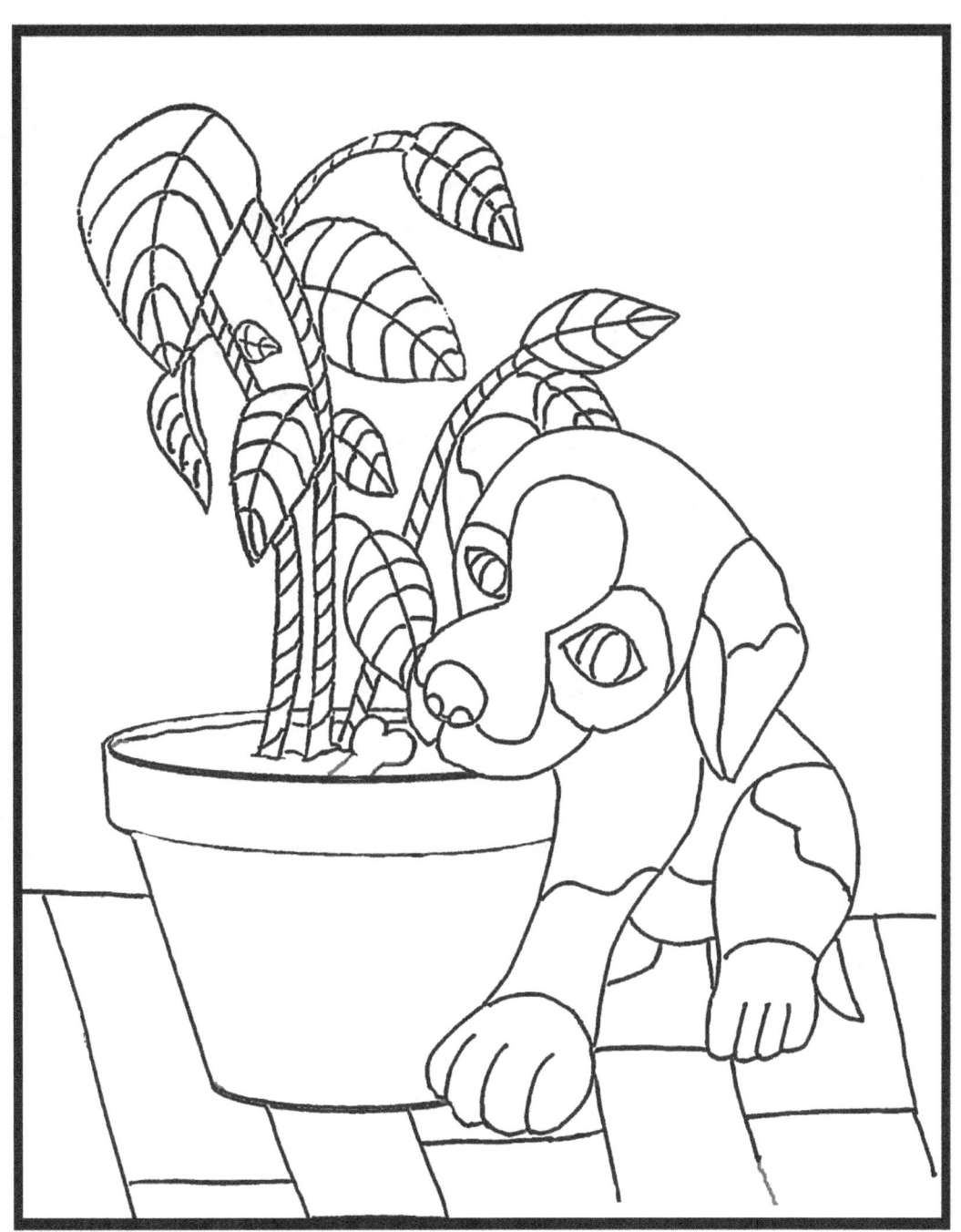

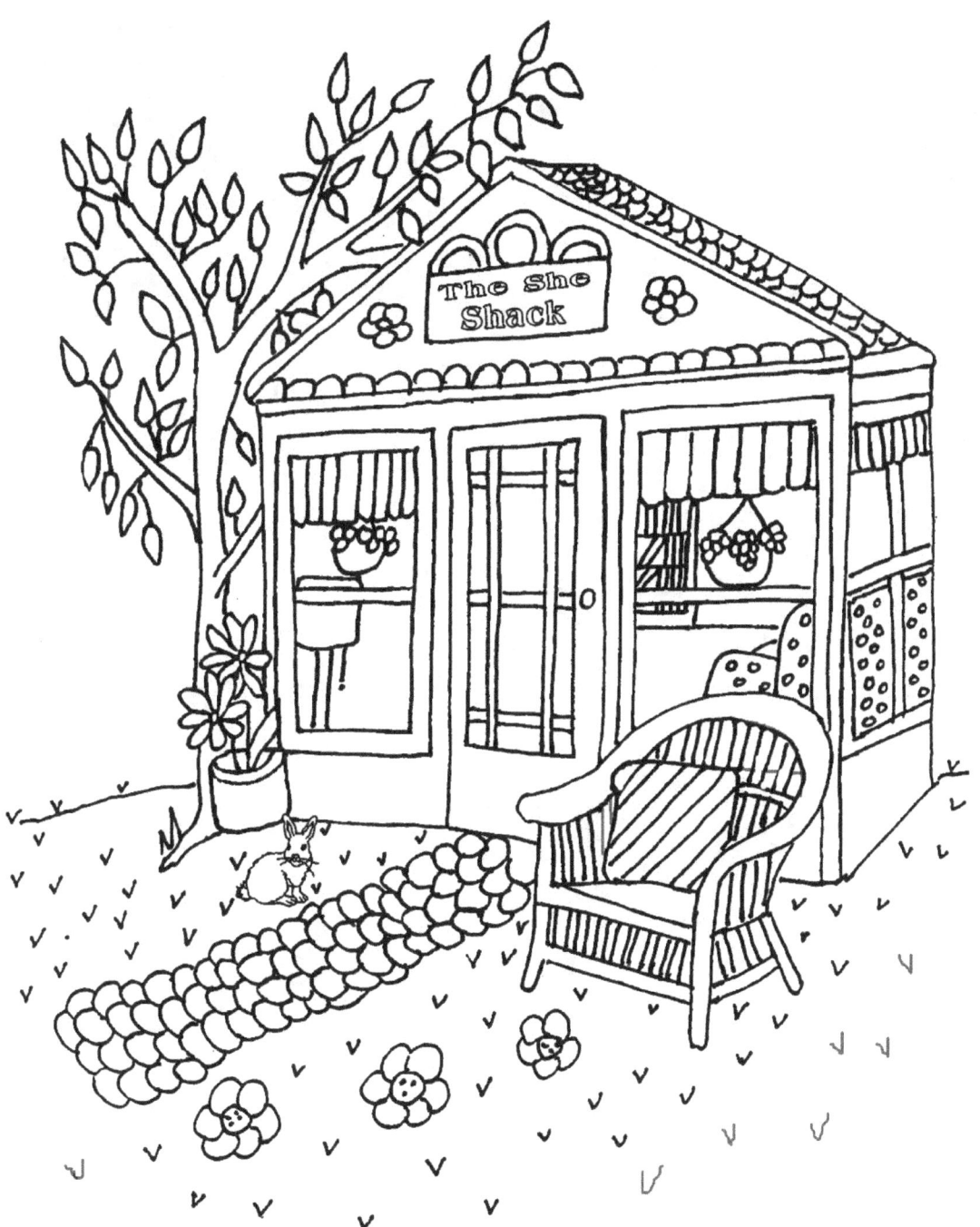

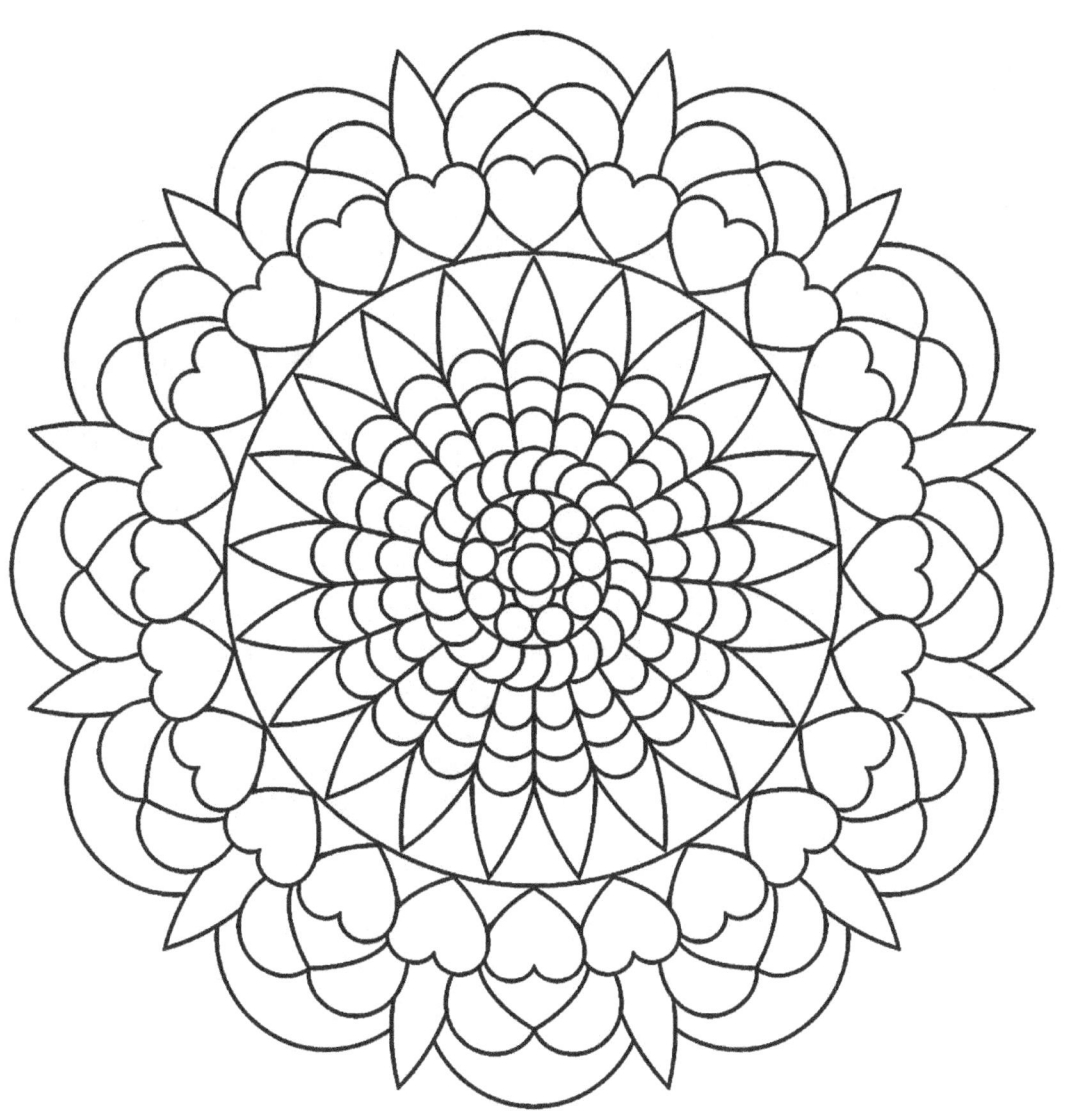

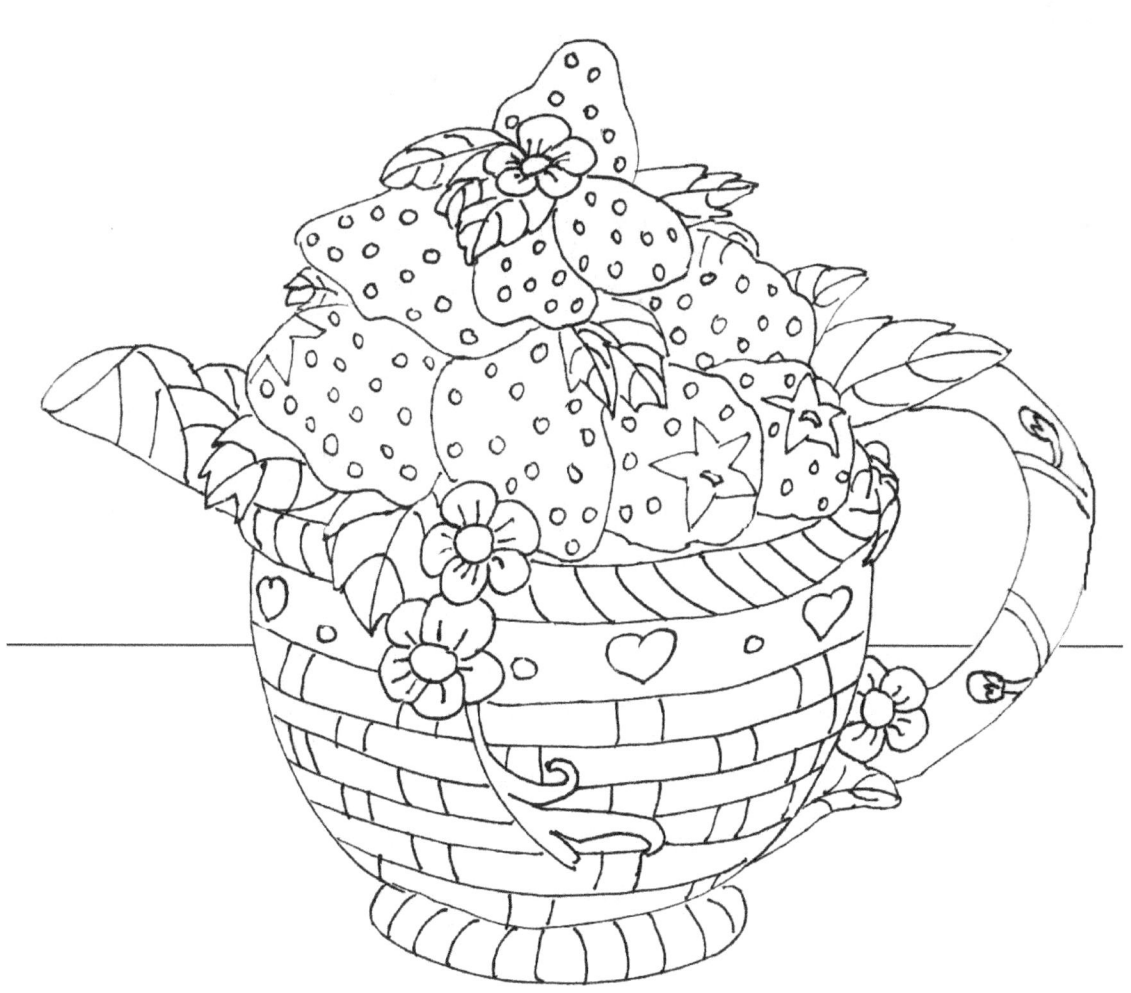

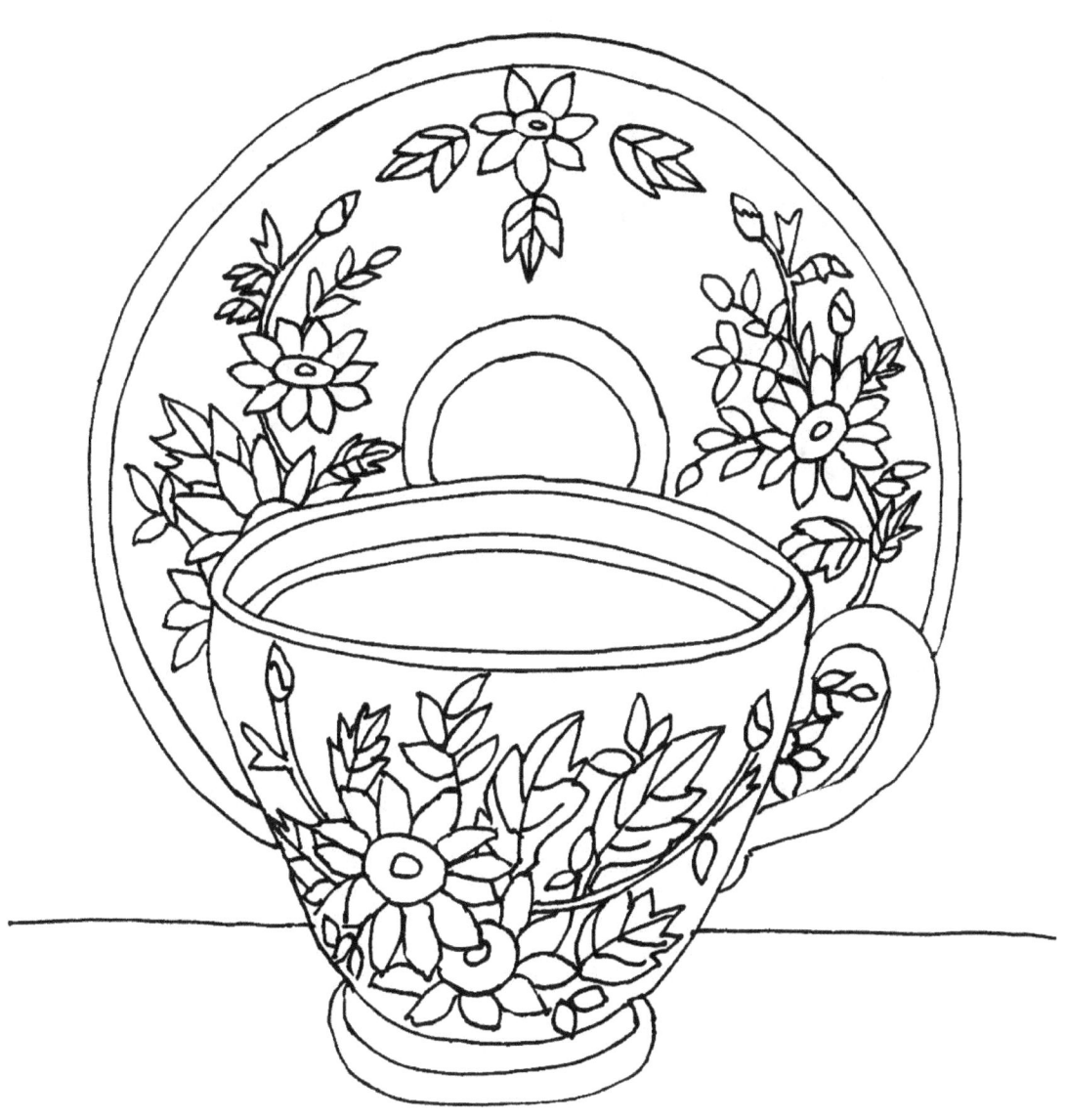

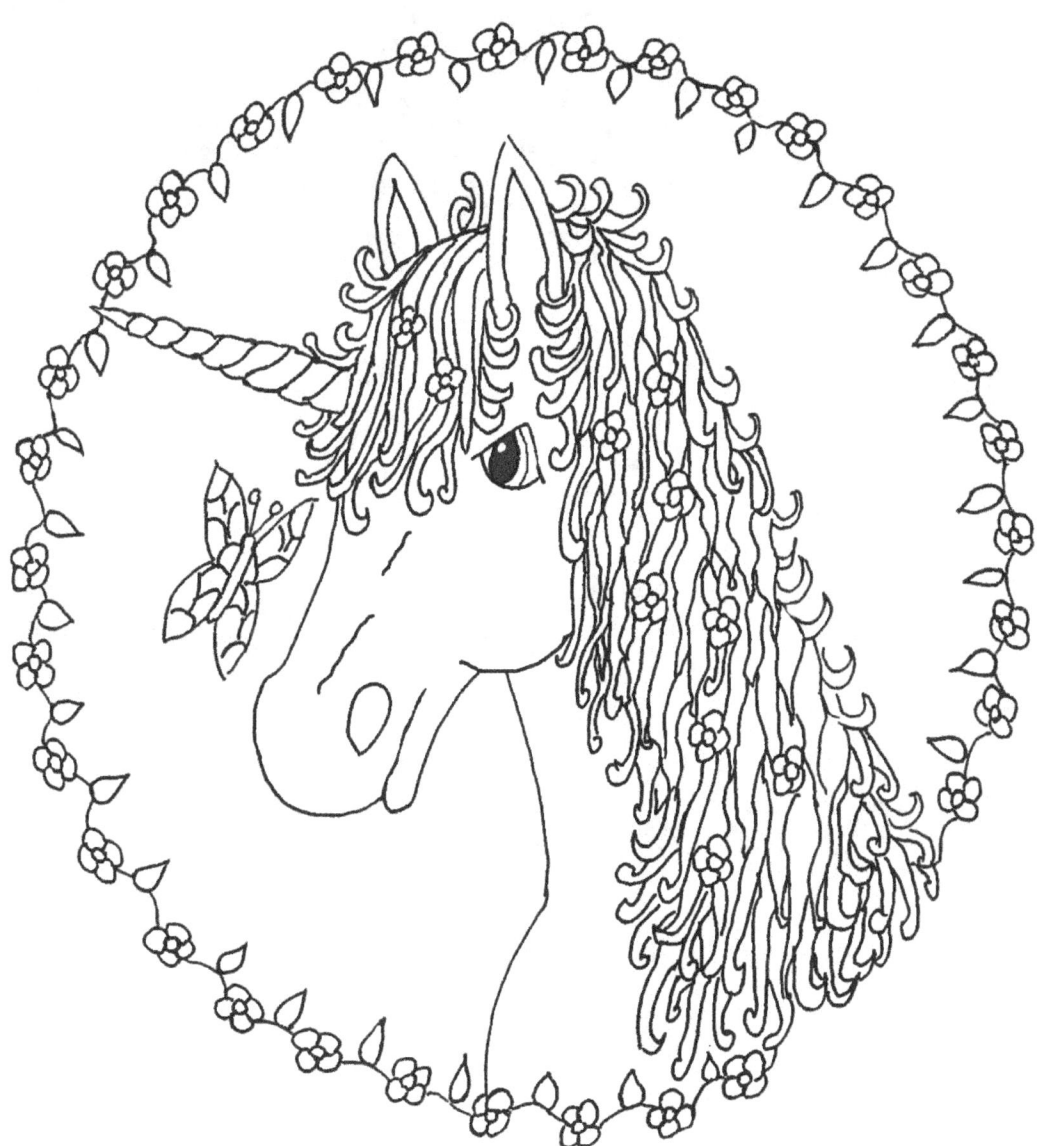

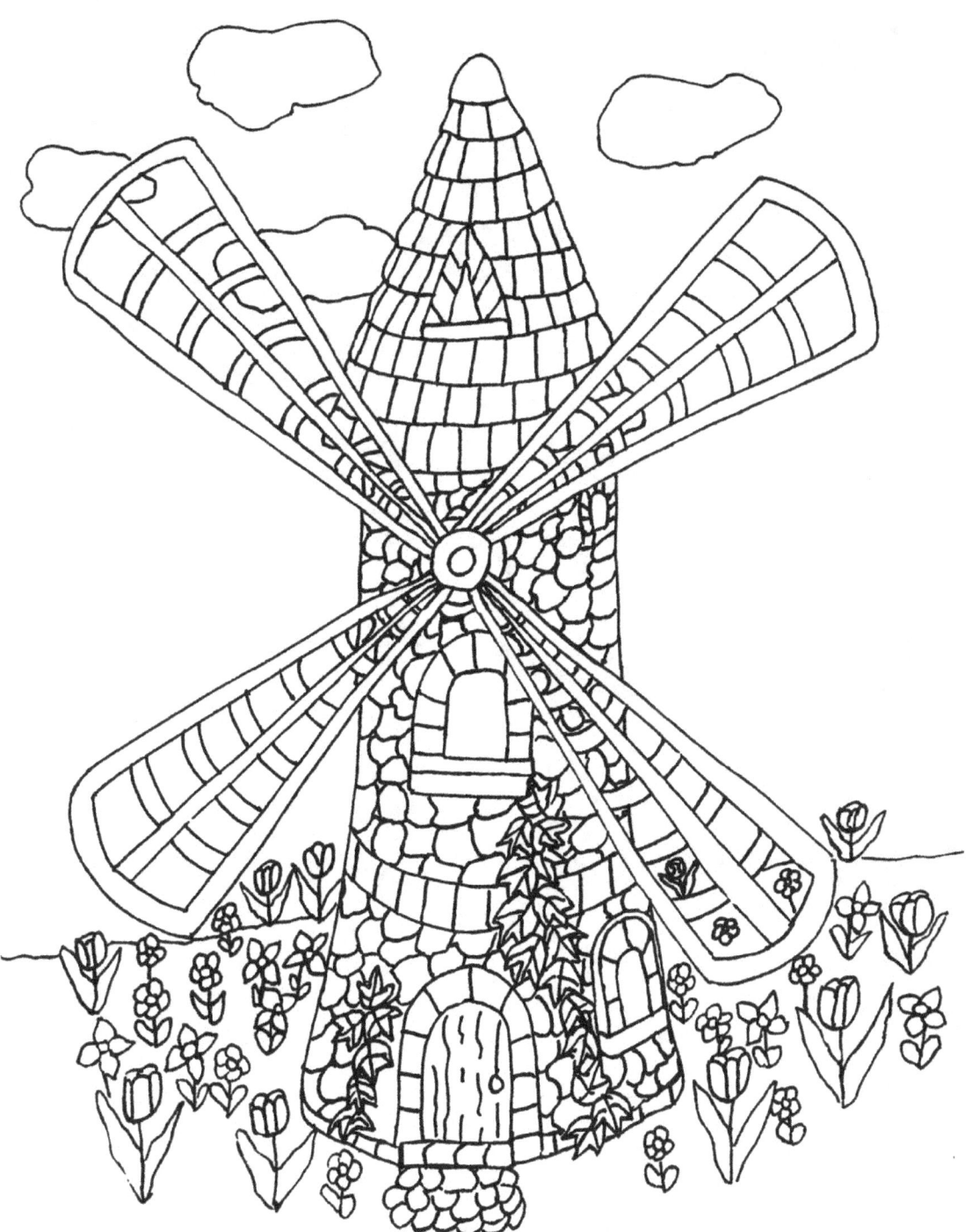

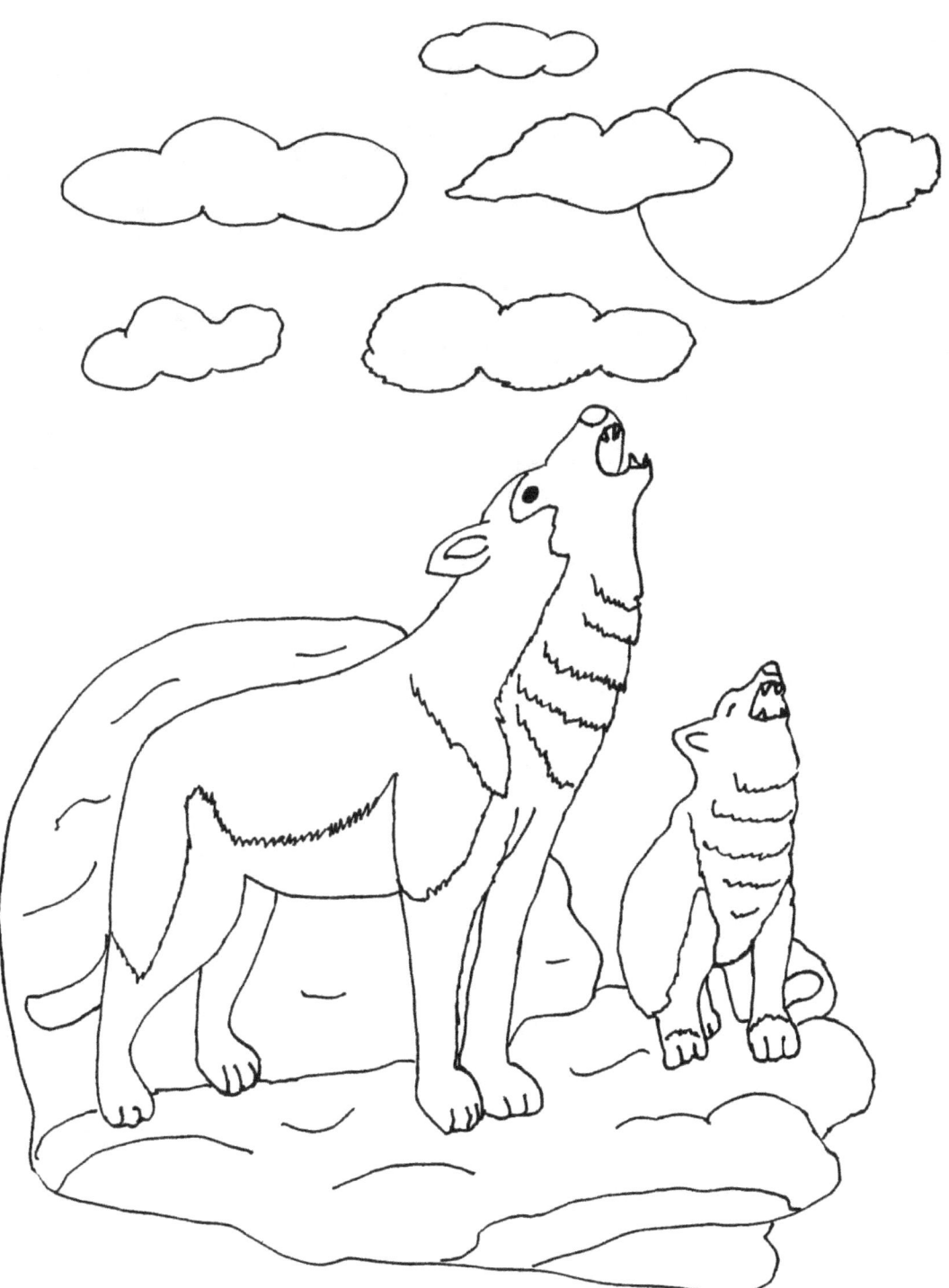